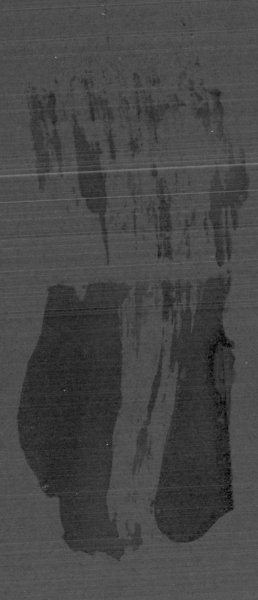

JUST IN TIME

Notes from My Life

Phyllis Newman

SIMON AND SCHUSTER
New York   London   Toronto   Sydney   Tokyo

With acknowledgment to
Irving, Joni, Alice, and Ron
without each of whom . . .

Simon and Schuster
Simon & Schuster Building
Rockefeller Center
1230 Avenue of the Americas
New York, New York 10020

Copyright © 1988 by Phyllis Newman

Published by the Simon & Schuster Trade Division

SIMON AND SCHUSTER and colophon are registered trademarks
of Simon & Schuster Inc.

Designed by: Levavi & Levavi
Manufactured in the United States of America

1　3　5　7　9　10　8　6　4　2

Library of Congress Cataloging in Publication Data

Newman, Phyllis.
Just in time.

1. Newman, Phyllis.　2. Television personalities—
United States—Biography.　I. Title.
PN1992.4.N39A3　1988　　791.45′092′4　[B]　　88-11566
ISBN 0-671-61880-6

Poem #1333 from *The Collected Poems of Emily Dickinson*, edited by Thomas H. Johnson, copyright
1914, 1942 by Martha Dickinson Bianchi. By permission of Little, Brown and Company.

The author is grateful for permission to reprint excerpts from:
"I'm Still Here" by Stephen Sondheim. Copyright © 1971, Range Road Music, Inc., Quartet Music,
Inc., Rilting Music, Inc. and Burthen Music Company, Inc. All rights administered by Herald Square
Music, Inc. Used by permission. All rights reserved.
"Mr. Goldstone" by Jule Styne and Stephen Sondheim. Copyright © 1959 by Norbeth Productions,

(continued at back of book)

For
Adolph, Adam, and Amanda,
Bobbie and Cynthia
and
My Mother and Father

A little Madness in the Spring
Is wholesome even for the King,
But God be with the Clown—
Who ponders this tremendous scene—
This whole Experiment of Green—
As if it were his own!

—Emily Dickinson

CURTAIN RAISER

September 1985

I am standing on the stage of Avery Fisher Hall at Lincoln Center wearing a black chiffon jacket and skirt trimmed in many-colored beading. Underneath the open jacket is a spaghetti-strapped matching camisole that, though modest by any standards, makes me feel like I'm wearing nothing, and that every spotlight, footlight, and jelled colored light has been brought in for the occasion to shine on me and my camisole.

Standing behind me are over a hundred men and women, the musicians of the New York Philharmonic orchestra, in black tie or gown. Facing me are three thousand or so New Yorkers who are passionate about the theater, including my children, Amanda and Adam. This audience is a mix of powerful producers, composers, designers, performers at every stage of their careers, corporate sponsors, fans, and live theater groupies.

They are standing and cheering. Waves of YEAHS! . . . WHAHS!
. . . FOOT STAMPING . . . HANDCLAPPING . . . HEADS WEAVING . . .
ARMS WAVING . . . I'm crying and laughing at the same time. My
left hand is grabbing George Hearn whose left hand is clutching
Lee Remick who's holding on to Mandy Patinkin who's kissing
Barbara Cook who's crying with Carol Burnett. My right hand is
swinging along with Elaine Stritch who's grinning at Lilianne
Montevecchi who's bowing gracefully with Adolph Green (my
husband of twenty-five years) who's deferring to Betty Comden
(his partner for fifty years). We had just finished performing a
concert version of James Goldman and Stephen Sondheim's brilliant show *Follies*. The live theatrical event of the season, *Follies*
was being recorded for an RCA Victor album and filmed for a
television documentary.

Follies, about a reunion of ex-Follies girls, takes place at a
theater that is about to be demolished. It touches on choices,
regrets, show business, marriage, family, talent, tradition, sur-
vival, and other things I haven't discovered yet.

> *Good times and bum times,*
> *I've seen 'em all and, my dear,*
> *I'm still here.*

This Is Your Life, Baby Phyllis . . . This Is *Your* Life.

ONE

One night my son Adam (age twenty-four, looks eleven) told me nervously that he was getting married.

Unlike the stereotype of another generation, I took it well. I was instantly transformed into an ice sculpture of a mother-in-law, suitable as a centerpiece for the buffet of a catered affair.

"Well, I'm . . . that is . . . Daddy and I are a little surprised."

"Actually, I told Dad."

I pulled the imaginary arrow out of my imaginary heart.

"I was nervous . . . Hell, I was scared out of my mind to tell you."

That jarred me a bit. He sure wasn't "scared as hell" to tell me he *wasn't* getting married or "getting any" during his four years at college. He used to call me several times a week, usually around twelve-thirty or one o'clock in the morning. His voice would be low and mournful. He would tell me in great detail his latest humiliation with Betsy or Nina or Sophie. As he got more and more worked up, he would invariably end with a plaintive, and penetrating, explanation.

"But, Mom, don't you understand? Not one girl I have ever liked has liked me back. Not one. Ever. They always want to be 'just friends.' I treat them courteously. I really respect them. I'm tender. But they don't want me. Not one. I guess that's the way it's always going to be."

I knew that he was exaggerating, but not lying. He was attractive, smart, funny, compassionate, and short. He and my husband and I (none of us tall) measured up against each other year after year.

I used all kinds of examples to reassure him.

"Well . . . you're the same height as Daddy and you're certainly taller than I am."

"It hardly stood in Daddy's way. He got me."

"It's just an exceptionally tall class this year at Harvard."

"Damn it! Look at Dustin Hoffman and Al Pacino. And they're not even good-looking."

"Every woman in the world would rather have Woody Allen than Robert Redford . . . All right, I go too far, but not that far. I have two words for you. Diane Keaton."

"Kerin said, 'God if only you were a little older' . . . no, no, it's not just that older women want to mother you."

"Set your sights lower . . . slightly. What I mean is that you always fall for tall, raving beauties. Try a small, medium one. Just for experience . . . I know I'm disgusting, I just don't know what to say anymore. This is going to change . . . I'm not Grandma. God, I wish she were here, she'd tell you and you'd believe her. I swear, your romantic and sexual life is going to be great. You've got everything . . . I'm *not* just trying to bolster you up . . . Well, I am. I'm supporting you with fact though, not fiction . . . Good. Call anytime, don't be a stranger. I sure do love you."

Not long before his graduation, we realized there was someone in his life who was female, well built, as they say, pretty, funny, vivacious, and extremely tall. She was crazy about our boy. Of course, he never told *us* the good news. He brought her to our house in the country and they stayed together in one room. We couldn't believe it. We never even got to have the discussion: "Do we *allow* it in *our own* house?" We were thrilled, to tell you the truth. From then on, his lack of desirability was not a topic. Now his troubles were in the "O.K. Corral of Life," and his self-confidence grew.

The next summer our daughter Amanda brought home a girlfriend of hers from school. She was a knockout from Brazil —intelligent, articulate, intense, sexy, and wonderful-looking. Aside from those qualities, she had little to recommend her. She was a free spirit who was about to start her junior year at the Sorbonne. Do you know the painting by Léger of a woman whose dominant feature is exaggerated wavy hair that covers one eye, one-third of her face, and a lot of the canvas? Well, that would be one version of this girl. She has unusually thick, long hair that falls over her eye a lot. Then she has to sweep it back with one hand, or maybe hold it back or up with two hands. She has what we used to call "bedroom eyes," a strong well-shaped nose that points down slightly, and a soft childish mouth. She's shorter than my son in the flat shoes she always wears. She has a perfect body and honey-colored skin. She's multilingual, from interesting families, and . . . *how could he do this to me?*

We weren't there for their meeting which, I gather, set off some sparks, "The Stars and Stripes Forever," sambas, and a minor earthquake. During the following year, he visited her in Paris, he met her parents in London, she came to New York when she had vacation, and they ran up major telephone bills. We knew they liked each other a lot, but it definitely was not our main concern, whatever that means. So it *was* a surprise. He told us on the evening before I was to leave for London on business. He and his "girl" timidly gave me her parents' phone number and address, and sort of said that her mother would be waiting for me to call when I arrived in London. It took me a day or two to get myself to call the "in-laws." Why? Because it was just all too grown up and real, and how could I have a son getting married when I haven't adjusted to my own marriage yet? Not enough preparation. Life was pushing ahead too fast, like the Fast Forward button on my internal remote control. At this rate the tape will . . . well, you know what I'm thinking.

I couldn't help it. I rewound the tape . . . two years.

May. A lady just going along singing a song, feeling good . . . feeling a . . . tiny lump under her arm.

Gynecologist: "Why don't you just go over and get a mammogram? It's probably nothing . . . Oh, say, in twenty minutes."

Mammographer's assistant speaking into waiting room: "Mrs. Phyllis Green, could you came back in, please?"

"What for?"

"Doctor needs another picture."

Lady to husband: "That's it."

Mammographer himself, in person, to both: "There's something a little suspicious. See?" (Lady blacks out with eyes open, head nodding.)

He points to a tiny constellation of whitish specks on the black-gray transparent picture of her left breast.

Mammographer to couple in stupor: "I'd like to think about it overnight and I'll call your doctor tomorrow. Relax."

Mammographer to husband with appropriate wink: "Go out and buy her a nice ice-cream soda."

Couple to bartender at Mortimer's, 10:30 A.M.: "Two double Bloody Marys, please; hold the tomato juice."

The next morning, very early, this same lady is lying alone in her big bed watching the phone light go on and off. She is afraid to take or make the calls herself. Her husband is in the other room at the phone, hearing and knowing. She feels suspended, empty, light. All her insides have been removed and replaced by terror. Her body is skin covering tunnels of fear. Finally, she jumps out of bed in her sweated nightgown and pulls open the door to that next room with fierce force.

To husband in someone else's voice: "Please, oh, please . . . What? . . . What?"

Her husband starts to talk gently. She lies down on the floor. She puts her mouth on the soiled rug and makes sounds that have no name, that can't and won't be described.

Lady to last of twelve doctors seen in two days: "My son is graduating from college next week. Can it wait until after that?"

That question triggered an associated memory that I didn't want to have then and I don't want now. But I have no choice, do I?

A few Mays earlier my friend, my girlfriend Felicia Montealegre Bernstein had gone through a similarly alarming medical scenario. At this same point in her story, after she had asked that same question word for word (just substitute daughter for son, same college), she called and asked me to have a cup of coffee with her. She came straight from the doctor's office. We met at a West Side coffee shop.

Felicia was a small and delicate, patrician blond Chilean beauty. I congratulate myself for having had her as a friend. She was discreet to the point of repression. She was intelligent and cultivated. A talented actress, musician, linguist, she had both wit and a clownish humor. She willingly gave up a lively career on television and the stage when she married Leonard Bernstein.

Her husband, the maestro, met my husband Adolph at summer camp. Lenny was a counselor. Adolph, too poor to be a camper, had come up as the guest of one, to be in a production of *The Pirates of Penzance*. Adolph had then, as now, a passion for classical music. He can sing everything from symphonies to violin solos. He knows the music note by note. He would like to sing it or hear it every moment. Each had heard a great deal about the other's gifts. They met and "eyed each other warily."

Lenny sat down to play some music for Adolph to identify. Adolph got the first two pieces easily. He listened to the third and confessed that he had no idea what it was. At that moment Lenny threw his arms around Adolph, hugged him, and admitted that he had just made it up to test him. Maybe that's not the most endearing way to begin a friendship, but they have been brotherlike friends ever since. They share not only music, but also the absolute sovereignty of Lewis Carroll. They went on to be fledgling "what they weres" together, then became successful at "what they did" around the same time, and collaborated with Betty Comden on their first show, *On the Town*, when they were in their mid-twenties.

I was introduced into the world of the Bernsteins in the late fifties when Adolph and I were getting semiserious about each other. He took me to one of Lenny's concerts at Carnegie Hall. We sat in the Bernstein box, close to the stage, keyboard side. I met Felicia who welcomed me warmly but reservedly. Her blond beauty was dazzling. She wore two strands of "good" pearls, sat up straight, and seemed like royalty to me. Lenny glanced up at the box at her before and after each piece of music.

Those early years with Adolph were a parade of firsts. This was the first concert I had gone to where I was going to meet the conductor, sit in his box, and later go to his house for a party. I don't remember what the music was because I didn't hear most of it. I kept staring at Felicia's small, champagne-colored satin evening purse . . . and at the enormous almost-genuine-leather black lump in my lap. Shoes to hair, she was all champagne and pearls.

I was more like a "two cents plain," chocolate syrup and seltzer . . . if we're going to keep liquid metaphors. I hadn't put myself together correctly that night because I was afraid of looking as if I had tried too hard, which I had. At the last minute I had taken off a sensible party frock and thrown on mismatched black separates. My style? Jersey City Anonymous.

We went backstage to the green room, where every bit of space and oxygen was taken by hypereffusive European types. Adolph and I were quickly led through them by one of Lenny's assistants and taken into his dressing room. That was where the family and the close friends went to talk about the concert and to kiss Lenny who sat at his dressing table—cooling down—in his bare chest with a towel draped around his neck, sipping scotch from his silver tumbler. Felicia stood next to him and welcomed everyone with warmth and radiance; her face couldn't make a wrong move. The atmosphere was festive and privileged. They seemed to have their own language, musical references, nicknames, and family jokes.

Lenny said, "Adolph, I thought of you through every single bar of that scherzo. I mean, it is just so . . . Adolph!" (Everyone nods in smiling agreement as the two men hug.)

"Koussi's tempi were quite a bit slower, no? . . . But eet was

Leonard and Felicia Bernstein with Adolph and me.

beautifool, Lenichki." (That from a frail, pale old lady, deferred to by all.)

I whispered, "Who is she?"

"Madame Koussevitzky."

"Oh . . . Who is Madame Koussevitzky?"

"Serge Koussevitzky's widow. He was a great conductor and Lenny's teacher and mentor."

"Oh."

From there we went across the street to the Bernsteins' apartment. They lived then with their children in the wonderful, ornate building, The Osborne, on the corner of Fifty-seventh Street and Seventh Avenue. The old-fashioned apartment was furnished comfortably with a charming individual style, but it was in no way "fancy" or "highly decorated."

I settled into a soft couch with a Coca-Cola, my drink of choice then. Felicia came and sat next to me and, in a natural, noncondescending fashion began our friendship with simplicity, laughter, and a shared exasperation at "those peculiar fellows." She sometimes corrected my grammar, or pronunciation, or hairstyle. We made fun of me and her, and I learned about style, food, fabrics, loyalty, and the sustenance that comes from culture.

Now, years later, in a West Side coffee shop, she's telling me about her diagnosis of breast cancer. She has that slightly distant look in her eyes, which I've come to know so well. And remember this is before every other word in print and on television is cancer, breast, tumor, colon. This is before "Doctor" Frank Field —a weatherman—urges you to call the cancer hot line, 1-800-CANCER, for more information. This is before Happy Rockefeller, Betty Ford, Nancy Reagan, and Truffaut, and AIDS. The jolt was bigger then, let me tell you.

"I asked the doctor; he didn't seem to think that a week would make any real difference. I can't bear to upset Jamie's graduation. I won't say a word until well after. Lenny agrees. Lenny is being so wonderful about it, and so . . . 'Lenny.' He's gone right to the head of the hospital. Oh, Phyllis. What a . . . thing."

And what a thing it was. From that moment on, her physical life deteriorated into death, and we never ever spoke another real word about her illness.

I don't mean that Felicia just up and died. Not at all. She had surgery, she got better, she looked well. A couple of summers later I was in a play in Stockbridge, Massachusetts, and her daughter Nina was nearby ushering at Tanglewood; Felicia came up with her son Alexander to visit. We were all having dinner at the authentically quaint Red Lion Inn; we were eating lobsters; we were laughing. I was describing how my son, Adam, who was an apprentice at the theater, was running the spotlight on my show. He was crouched on a tiny catwalk above the audience working the light from there. On the opening night, when it came time for my big solo song (the show was *I Married an Angel,* the song was "I'll Tell the Man in the Street"), the stage lights dimmed, the spot didn't come on, and I was singing in darkness. I looked up to the catwalk and saw my son sound asleep. I finished the number in semishadow, and walked offstage cursing Dr. Spock and his "spare the rod" routine.

The kids went off to meet friends and left us at the table. Felicia told me that she had some back pain that probably came from a pinched nerve, but that there *was* some little shadow on the X ray. She didn't want to frighten her children, but had really come up to tell her youngest daughter, Nina, what was going on in case she had to go back into the hospital. I told her I knew she was fine. She agreed. End of conversation. Her choice.

The rest of her terrible days I have turned into a nonsequential, unspecific, sorrowful blur. I simply can't remember, I won't remember, I can't forget. Shopping with her as if in slow motion —cotton sheets, cotton nightgowns, imported, fine, everything for the bed. Coming up to visit her directly from the opening night of my one-woman show in New York. She had a nurse. She was using all her "all cottons." She was watching "Laurel and Hardy" on television. Lenny was with her. I told her about the show. She was receptive and loving and happy I was there, and gone already, to me. I prepared for her death because I didn't know what else to do.

I'd never had a friend die on me. My father and then my mother died on me. I still don't know what to do about any of them. I thought a girlfriend would talk to you about what she was feeling, what she wanted, what she had learned. Ingrid Bergman would have. Years before Felicia and I had made a home movie at her house in Connecticut—a parody of the Bette Davis/Joan Crawford horror flick, *Whatever Happened to Baby Jane?* Steve Sondheim wrote, directed, and photographed it. Ours was called "Whatever Happened to Felicia Montealegre?" Felicia played a beautiful young ballerina, and I her ugly, stooped, jealous sister who accompanied her on the piano. The film opened with a montage of Felicia dancing madly intercut with cheering crowds. We pan to the floor. I have thrown banana peels all over. Felicia dances delicately and avoids them. It pans up to me eating more and more bananas and getting sicker and sicker. Finally, she trips. Horror! Cut to me at the piano maniacally playing with my elbow and nose at breakneck speed. I have foiled my sister. She is in a wheelchair and I have become blond and beautiful and a star pianist. There are many short scenes of my torturing her with food, and of my mad piano playing and singing. A stranger comes into our midst, played by Lenny. He disrupts our strange relationship; he pays too much attention to Felicia. I plot to kill her by rolling her down hills and dales and drowning her in the swimming pool. By a strange quirk of fate and cinema magic, it is I who am maimed and we three live unhappily ever after as a crippled musical trio called The Norns. The movie was brilliantly shot by Steve. We did it all in one day. Felicia, Lenny, Adolph (he had a cameo as the deus ex machina), and I worked like hell. We changed clothes and wigs and makeup. We rented a wheelchair. We had a wonderful time.

Now it is many years later. We are all together at a newly bought and hastily furnished house on Long Island, as Felicia always called East Hampton. Her thick blond hair is now in a skimpy crew cut because of her medication, but her beauty is undiminished. We decide to play a word game, the Bernstein family and all of us. It is both a relaxing and competitive pastime that we share, that connects us all. We're playing, we're laughing, we forget for a minute what's happening. Julia, the house-keeper, says, "Dinner is ready." We all get up, we look at Felicia

Felicia.

to see if she wants assistance because she is in a wheelchair. She waves us away as only she and royalty can. She smiles that smile and says, "Whatever *did* happen to Felicia Montealegre?"

God, this is depressing me, so I can just imagine what it's doing to you. Cancer, my dear, is no laughing matter, no small feat, leaves no stone unturned, and certainly is no way to treat a lady!

You become a member of a not-too-exclusive and not-too-stimulating club. The Mastectomy Chapter is a particularly large one and a particularly bum one. We're sort of all-knowing with each other. We cheerlead, pep each other up, sympathize, and pretend that we're all right, good as new, getting over it, in the majority, lucky it wasn't worse, superior, inferior . . . who really knows?

I apologize for the detours. I'm walking down a long hall with many doors . . . I'm opening them one by one, taking a look inside, leaving them open, going back to the hall and proceeding at a snail's pace. At this rate, it will take me such a long time to come to the end of the corridor and into what? A large, sun-filled living room? A theater filled with an adoring audience? A step, and then blackness, a woeful descent? More likely, more corridors.

The corridors are filled with surprises. It never occurred to me that a child of mine would graduate from Harvard or Brown. I didn't dream of it one way or another. But I was thrilled when both my son and daughter got into their first choice. They wanted it very much, therefore I wanted it for them. Adolph and I always made it clear to them that we were not in the "You're going to get everything we could never afford" business. We both knew that our talent, drive, intellect, or lack of it had little to do with the amount of money spent on us as children.

Nevertheless . . . nevertheless . . . the old mom and pop were pretty excited to be able to watch our baby boy get his diploma and a prestigious prize for writing. That was the main event.

But, the not-so-sub subtext was that I was going to go into the hospital for the surgery the minute I got back to New York. But, since I was going to be in Boston, I had gotten the name of a great breast cancer specialist at Massachusetts General Hospital for yet another opinion. Along with my mother-of-the-graduate duds I was carrying around a large manila envelope with my mammogram in it. Every time I saw it in my drawer under my bras and panties, I got spooked. I know, I know . . . it was perverse to put it there. But tell me, do you or do you not almost always put things of many descriptions in the top drawer under your underwear?

I went to see this charming old doctor, who was famous for recommending lumpectomies instead of mastectomies. He took a great deal of time with me. He was gentle, he examined me, he studied those ugly pictures, and his conclusion was that it was possibly cancer in situ, that is, it hadn't become a tumor or a real cancer yet, and that there was no rush for surgery.

Without exchanging a word, Adolph and I knew that just wasn't so. That doctor made me feel good, and he believed his diagnosis, because he sent a copy of it to my New York doctor, but he was wrong.

Because of so many graduations around the city, we could only get one large room at the hotel in Boston. Adolph, our daughter Amanda, my niece Bonnie, and I had to share it and its one bathroom. It added to the college weekend atmosphere, but it didn't give me a hell of a lot of privacy in which to agonize over my impending date.

A few of the parents who lived in or near Boston gave parties and we got to meet some of Adam's classmates and their families from all over the world. There was shared appreciation of how good life had been to some of us, that we were able to come together for this occasion. This is not, as you will see, the story of a lush, but it was very necessary for me to drink vodka, slowly and steadily, throughout these evenings, so I could take my mind off myself. I admit I'm hyperdramatic, and I did imagine that everything I was doing was for the last time.

GIDGET GROWS UP AND DIES

Gidget is played by Margaret Sullavan. Everyone admires Gidget for her pluck, we see her laughing and being gay at parties. She insists on having her picture taken with her family constantly. Zoom into photo—smiling mouth, sad eyes. We see her drying her eyes as her son gets his diploma. Wait a minute . . . something's going on . . . the president of Harvard is leaving the stage . . . he's walking down the aisle, resplendent in his gown and cap of many tassels . . . he has a giant-size diploma in his hand . . . he stops at Gidget's seat . . . she looks around bewildered . . . her blond curls are bewildered—they're tossing back and forth. The president speaks: "THIS IS FOR YOU, GIDGET GREEN, A DIPLOMA FROM THE COLLEGE OF LIFE AND WONDERFULNESS . . . FOR THE BRAVEST LITTLE FUCKER OF A MOTHER IN ALL OF HARVARD."

This is a note I found just before I handed in my final version of this book.

"This is May 18 and yesterday I discovered a 'lump' under my left arm and I'm scared to death, and I have a . . . what's the opposite of stiff? . . . lax . . . soft . . . crumpled . . . slack . . . I guess slack upper lip. No character . . . no moxie . . . and what's really disgusting is that 'First You Cry,' the TV movie based on Betty Rollins's moving book about her 'bout' with breast cancer, is on the TV. . . . And guess what masochistic creep is going to watch it? It just started, and scared and slightly drunk and crazed as I am . . . I have to laugh. I'll do the sequel when I'm *fine*, called 'First You Laugh.' "

That was May 1983, and I wasn't "fine." No one is completely sure why, but spring and the month of May in particular seem to be the time that a disproportionate number of breast cancer cases are diagnosed. It's the season for trees' sap . . . hormonal uprisings . . . rebirth . . . and accelerated internal motions.

I had two shocking Mays, and then two more filled with apprehension, distress, fear, emotional and physical discomfort.

Then in the fifth May, twenty-five years to the day that I'd got my first, came my second Tony Award nomination, for Aunt Blanche in Neil Simon's *Broadway Bound*. And now in this, the sixth (but who's counting?), comes this book that I've been writing and living for so long. I hope that my good fortune offers encouragement and cyclical *good* news to those who may also have received bad news.

Maybe this just looks like I'm trying to be oh so noble and oh so inspirational. All right, but here's the straight skinny. I can be the fastest, freshest mouth in the East, and I'm still constantly astonished by life. I want to keep fighting back or giving back, depending on how nice it's being to me at that moment. I'm still sore as hell, but I don't think I'd have it any other way.

Am I a better person? Not on your life. Am I a nicer person? I was pretty nice to begin with. Am I in a position to help and interest and amuse people? Yes. Am I trying? Looking? Yes. Is it working? Sometimes . . .

TWO

Are there any questions? I don't want to be interrupted once I begin. All right, I guess there's no way you're just going to keep quiet, and let me tell my story the way I want to. So I'll just talk fast, and we'll see what happens.

Everyone thought I was a midget. I thought I was a kid. I was around six years old and doing a Carmen Miranda act between showings of the movie *King's Row* at a vaudeville theater in New Jersey. I know . . . who was Carmen Miranda? . . . What was *King's Row*? Don't worry. I'll explain later. Let me be the judge of what is important, pertinent, impertinent. Trust me.

My costume was blinding red satin. I wore a turban with different-colored feathers sticking out of it like a dust mop, a brief bralike top over my nonexistent bosom . . . over my nonexistent bosom . . . Why am I saying that twice? That's how it comes out. The skirt was tight over the hips, with a cascade of ruffles to the floor. It had a wide split down the middle which revealed my truly unformed legs.

My father would walk out from the wings to the upright piano

23

at the side of the stage as soon as "The End" flashed on the movie screen. Garish red and blue lights came up and he would start playing your regulation 1940s South American vamp. Then, I sambaed on, all no foot three of me, and sang my tiny heart out. I rolled my *r*'s just like Carmen.

"Ow would you lahk to spend a weekend een 'avana? Ow would you lahk to see the Carrrr-eeeee-beeean shore?" They laughed when I wanted them to. I wasn't a joke. I sang and danced well, my patter was amusing, they got their money's worth if you throw in the movie.

My poor daddy played my musical arrangements very badly. He wasn't much of a pianist, but he made my whole career as Baby Phyllis possible. He invented me, along with hypnotizing cats, hand-painted hats, and a fortune-telling mother, so let's not look a gift daddy in the . . . well . . . at least not too closely . . . yet.

The first time I sang in Atlantic City was 1939. That year my mother was known as Marvelle and was reading palms at the Merry-Go-Round Bar of the Ritz Carlton Hotel. My father was called Dr. S. A. Newman or Gabel the Graphologist, and he was analyzing handwriting at an open stand on the boardwalk. We were just your ordinary all-American family trying to make a buck in the summer before the "Big War."

My father's stand looked like . . . well, let's see. Do you remember carnival stands where you threw the ball at the stacked wooden milk bottles, or shot the nice little man and his ducks as they went back and forth making the clang-chika-chika-ring sounds? Well, it was like those, but only four or five feet wide and deep enough for one man and possibly his child to stand comfortably. It had a high counter so you could lean on your elbow while you tried to write a brief message and your name unselfconsciously and normally, so my father could analyze it.

When I hung out there, I'd be lifted up onto the counter. I'd sit there for hours watching the people go by on the boardwalk, watching my daddy do his "work" at this funny little spot. It

During my reign as Miss Atlantic City, Jr.

wasn't brilliantly decorated. The facts were painted on the front with some stars scattered among the words. On the expanse of white painted wood behind my father's head there were photographs of him with Jack Dempsey, Gene Tunney, and the Three Stooges.

July 1939
I don't know what to write.

Mary Corcoran

My father bent over the piece of paper with a magnifying glass

and said, "You see the way you don't quite finish the last letter
of each word? See, the *T* and the *W*? They're incomplete. That
shows a problem with seeing things through. You're a dreamer.
You start a lot of things and then you lose interest, probably in
romance too. I see a somewhat flighty romantic person in your
writing."

The stout, graying Mary Corcoran in her sensible cotton print
dress, sandals, and stockings looked puzzled. "Gee, I don't think
that's so. I've been a nurse for almost twenty years. I've hardly
ever missed a day. No . . . No . . . I would say I'm the opposite.
Yes, exactly the opposite from what you're saying." She was beginning to get upset. "I'm *too* dedicated, *too* conscientious. I don't
go to sleep until my house is spotless and I've called all my
relatives and friends who are alone, prayed for their souls, and
laid out a nice clean uniform for the next morning."

Daddy was not a terribly good judge of character.

He said: "I see. Yes, but . . . I bet it all goes out the window
with men, huh? I just bet you're a little terror with those doctors,
huh? Those good-looking doctors."

Mary Corcoran kept opening and closing the catch of her
sensible white vinyl purse. "I don't think you know what you're
doing. This is ridiculous. Just give me my dollar back. I never
believed in any of this . . . garbage. I thought, oh well, it's my
vacation. I never should have . . . Just give me my dollar back."

"You don't understand. This shows the real you . . . underneath. Your handwriting doesn't lie. We know these things.
Relax. I see other things. Your *o*'s are very open, very full,
there's going to be a big change in your life. Just open up like
your *o*'s and a small blond man with an *o* in his name will want
to spend a lot of time with you. Don't give up. . . . Now, your *g*'s
are very interesting . . . "

"Keep the dollar. . . . Thank you, I've had enough. Why is that
child staring at me? She's too young to be hanging around a
place like this."

I said, "That's my daddy and he's very good. You should listen
to him. He can do anything. He knows everything."

"It's O.K., honey . . . Look, Mary, tell your friends about me,
O.K.? The rest of the nurses at the convention . . . I'll do a dis-

count for ten or more. They'll have fun. Here's my card. Enjoy your stay. Everyone's writing tells a different story."

As Mary left, she looked at us as if we were the oddest pair she'd ever seen. I said, "Don't worry, Daddy . . . I didn't like her anyway. I bet a lot of people will come up after they leave the beach."

He crumpled up the piece of paper with her "sensible" note and kept it inside his fist as he banged on the counter. He stopped himself, threw the paper down, and said, "Come on, it's going to be slow for a while. I'll buy you a soda." He lifted up part of the counter to get out, then he took me down. He put the pads and pencils in the pocket of his short-sleeved shirt and put up a sign: THE DOCTOR WILL BE BACK IN HALF AN HOUR.

He asked the souvenir man who had the other half of the stand to keep an eye on things. What things? We went down the block off the boardwalk to a "shoppe." He had coffee and a toasted English with lots of butter. I had a chocolate milk shake.

I don't remember how I felt about him then. Was I embarrassed or just sad? Did I feel both superior and threatened? Or did I think he was the greatest daddy in the world? I hope so.

I was with my father because I had a day off from Daddy Dave's revue "Hollywood Screen Test," and my momma had to work that afternoon. There was an "affair" at the hotel where she worked. They were having a luncheon party for some executives who were there with a business convention. Usually she told fortunes and read palms at night only, at the Merry-Go-Round Bar. But the banquet manager had hired her to "read" anyone there who might want it. I guess they paid her a small flat fee and she made money on the tips.

Momma was very attractive that year, her thirty-ninth. Her hair was wavy and dark blond. She was just beginning to be plump. She wore rayon crepe dresses mostly in blue with big shoulder pads and plunging necklines. Her nails and lips were dark bluish red. She always had a charming flirty quality until anyone took her remotely seriously. She had that nonaccent accent and why can't I remember her voice? The thing is she was not a fake, she really wasn't. You'll wind up believing me.

"What do you see in that ball, miss? . . . " He picks up the triangularly folded shiny card from the center of the table. "Hell, I can't read your name without my glasses."

"Marvelle." My mother laughs a soft musical laugh and looks down into a small crystal ball. "I don't see anything at the moment. You look into it, and really concentrate on what you *want* me to see."

The man looks slightly uncomfortable, but Marvelle's manner is relaxed and sure. They both look intently into the ball. She closes her eyes for a moment. She opens them and keeps them on the ball.

"Who's . . . R? . . . I see an R who's very strong, very important to you. But there's some trouble with R . . . Yes, I see trouble recently." She looks up at him. "Do you know an R? Do you have an R close to you?"

The man doesn't answer for a few moments. He stares at Marvelle. His face and eyes go from middle-age genial to American tough to little boy, loose and watery.

"An R? . . . Yes. That's very good. Yes . . . very good." He's deciding whether to go on with it, whether to reveal himself to this stranger, this fortune-teller. He laughs, but it would not stand up in a court of law.

"What else do you see? Do you see anything else more concrete . . . about this . . . R?"

My mother looks at the man. She says gently: "You should say good-bye to her. It's never going to work out. You're never going to give up . . . everything . . . everyone else, and R is beginning to make other plans. She *is* seeing someone else."

The man is startled. He doesn't know whether to go on, or simply kill my mother on the spot. Well, just in case she's on the level, he says, "Who? Can you see *who* that someone else is?"

"Put your fingers on the ball and really concentrate."

"Christ! *I* don't *know* who it is, if I did I wouldn't . . . "

"*Please, relax, help me.* Put your mind on things you want solved. Concentrate."

Instead of touching it lightly, he grabs the crystal ball as if he were about to shoot a basket from center court. There's no room on it for my mother's fingers. She looks at him. His eyes are squeezed shut and he's holding on.

She says, "Everything is going to work out for the best. She cares about you very much. But she's just being sensible. You'll feel better once this is settled, you'll be relieved . . . I see some problems around the leg . . . the knee . . . "

"Oh my God!"

"Don't have surgery. You don't need it. It will clear up on its own. I see . . . " She closes her eyes again for a moment; he can't stop looking at her. "Yes . . . Bill . . . Is that your name, Bill? (He nods yes.) Bill . . . It's possible that R will move to where her friend is. I don't think you know him. Or maybe you've met him. He's older . . . Yes . . . She won't be around. I don't see her around. I see you . . . I see good things, good health, yes, good things. Listen to me . . . let her go."

She opens her eyes and puts her hands in her lap. Bill grabs my mother's hands and kisses them. This doesn't embarrass her. Men and women often have to touch her, to thank her, to feel her realness, to hide their amazement, to have an extra few moments to decide what their next move should be. Do they listen to her? Do they believe her? Is it a trick? Was she just lucky this time? Should they tip her? How much? Should they hire her? Who is this woman? Why is she doing this? She's refined. A little showy yet terribly ladylike and reserved. Attractive. She has no come-ons. No stories. She says nothing about herself. She always tells men, if they ask, that she's married, happily married, and has three gorgeous daughters. Two of them already grown up. Her regulars at night see her husband hanging around a back table at the club. He never takes his eyes off her. His body tenses and he starts walking around if a man sits too long with her. It tenses only slightly less if it's a woman.

"Ray (he called her Ray, or the Yiddish version of Rachel . . . Rucchhel—guttural) . . . you should only give them ten minutes . . . tops. This way they'll come back. Those old bags take advantage of you. They have nothing else to do but hang around."

This is not a first-time exchange. Variations on this theme are recurrent. It always gets to my mother. He has to do it. They play it out.

"Sig, please! Why do you watch me? Why do you time me? I can't stand it. I spend as much time as I have to. I help them. They keep coming back because I help them. They pay me. *They pay me,* Sig!"

Now the nerve has been uncovered and poked at in both of them. Is that the spot where the cancer that killed both of them was nurtured? Is that what it does? Is that how it works? I don't know, but it feels like that to me now.

My father's anger is uncontrollable, my mother can't stop. She's crying.

"A lot of them want to be my friends. They're good to me, Sig. They'd do anything for me. You never understand. You never let anyone be my friend. Not anyone. You're jealous!"

My father is not crying. He is screaming. He has a vein that comes straight down the middle of his thin-skinned forehead. It is enlarged. It looks like a blue thermometer.

"*Jealous! Jealous!* Of a fortune-teller! You sit there pushing your shoulders at them, laughing, flirting with them, trying to make me look like a fool. You think I don't see what you're doing? Always belittling me. Making me feel like nothing. I taught you this. I taught you everything. You should *pay me*! You were an ignorant greenhorn. You . . . you and your snooty selfish family . . . they never liked me. You've held me back. You're always holding me back. I can't trust you. *I can't trust anyone!*"

"*Sig, please. The baby . . . shah . . . Sig . . . shah . . . please!*"

I cried in my room, in my bed, in the dark every time I heard them. I "vowed" that when I grew up, I would never fight with anyone, especially my husband and children. Well . . . they are practically the only people I do have knock-down-drag-outs with. So, there's absolutely no lesson to be learned from all this.

Do you know what the Steel Pier was like in 1939 when it was the "showplace of the nation" and "a vacation in itself"? It was this rambling Disneyland-like show business fantasy on a long,

long pier under which the Atlantic Ocean did its number, with spotlights on it. I could wander around freely, day or night . . . well, not too late. My parents were strict about bedtime and getting proper sleep.

There were three or four "feature photoplays" playing at all times in different parts of the pier. I saw them all, or at least parts of them all. Sometimes I'd wander into three movies in one hour, because I was a little kid and it was fun. There were six big fun houses, an Eskimo Village, some kind of ballet. There were a lion tamer, diving horses, and various animals on display in cages. My father arranged for me to pose with anything and anyone. One picture shows me in a lion tamer's costume holding a big whip and a tiny stool as my weapon. The lion is looking at me without interest from the safety of his cage. On a hastily painted (by Daddy) placard in front of the cage, it says:

FEARLESS PHYLISS
WILD ANIMAL TRAINER!

It was the time when big bands were big attractions, and the well-known ones played the pier for dancing all day. I'd stand smack up against the bandstand, in the huge central, open, wooden-floored ballroom. I'd watch and dance around alone for hours or however long I had between my own shows. I watched Gene Krupa's nonstop drumming and never-closed mouth. I sang along with Frank Sinatra and the Harry James band from my little solo corner of the dance floor. I don't remember if I met them. I guess my father took me around to all the stars who were playing the pier. I only remember meeting the ones with whom I have pictures. Many of those names are forgotten now. They were dazzling to me then, and were one hell of a "photo opportunity" for my publicity maven daddy.

I am grinning, very nonneurotically, with a tooth or two missing in most of the pictures, so I guess I was pretty happy. Other kids were building sand castles on the beach, I was hobnobbing, or at least posing with singers, with "acts," with animals, Sharkey the Wonder Seal, with Miss Atlantic City, Jr. losers (I was the winner), with John Boles and Bruce Cabot, the Three Stooges (I had a crush on Larry's son), Lo Hite and Stanley, opera star (for a minute) Marion Talley, all of the Ben Yost singers in their hats and clown suits (and a hat on me), oh, and Jack Haley, the Tinman from the *The Wizard of Oz* (he looked a lot like my daddy).

I was the youngest and smallest kiddie in *Daddy Dave's Kiddie Revue*. The others were fairly hulking teenagers in terrible costumes and makeup, who tapped, acrobated, sang, recited, played saxophones, and did bad magic in "Hollywood Screen Test." We did four shows a day and five on the weekends. I wore my own modest short white sharkskin dress and sang two of my proven socko songs which rarely failed to stop the show. The kids hated me. I loved them. I wanted to hang out with them, play with them, and be them. They simply wouldn't have me. They were too old and too "pro" for me. So I played around and explored the vast Steel Pier alone.

That summer Belle Baker was playing one of the big clubs in Atlantic City. Belle was a good, schmaltzy singer who had been popular in vaudeville and clubs in the twenties and thirties. Somehow she got to know my parents. Did my mother "read" her? Probably. Of course, that must have been the connection.

One night, it was set up that I would sing for her in the Round the World Room of the President Hotel. She was sitting ringside with my parents and some of her family, including her young niece Marilyn Cooper. Marilyn was about my age—small and dark, with enormous mournful brown eyes. I had rehearsed with the band that afternoon. I was in the middle of my second or third song and "selling it" for Belle. I could tell that she was excited; she was applauding and clucking like my mother. Then I noticed a small figure get up from Belle's table and make her way through the white circle of the spotlight across the dance floor and up to the little platform in front of the band where I was singing behind a big microphone. Soon she was standing next to me. I kept singing and looking at her sideways. She stood there. I tried to ignore her and carry on. Finally, she pushed me off the platform. Yes, she simply put her hands on my arm and

In "Hollywood Screen Test," I got to wear my white sharkskin dress and sing two songs.

pushed me. She didn't hurt me, I didn't fall, there was just no room for me and her. The band stopped, and then Marilyn started singing her own song. I hate to tell you, but she sang great . . . a trumpet for a voice, which she still has. After her short song she told the astonished group: "I'm Belle Baker's honest to God niece—that kid is just a stranger. I'm the one who should be here."

I guess she was right, I guess she hated my little guts. I think that I was so used to being the little star that I didn't doubt for a second that I would prevail. I have no idea what was in "Auntie" Belle's mind, but next thing I knew, I was called Baby Phyllis Baker, Belle Baker's protégée, and I was booked into the very same club . . . for money.

At certain times I thought I was the luckiest kid in the whole world. I felt as though I owned Atlantic City. The entire President Hotel, the boardwalk, and the beach were my personal playground until about nine-thirty. That was when I would finish performing my "Baby Phyllis" act. (The dinner show only; I was six and couldn't stay up too late.) Then we had to go home. You see, we didn't actually stay at the hotel, but at a rooming house a few blocks away. All in one room with kitchen privileges, which meant we could use the stove and had one shelf in the communal icebox. I don't remember much about eating there; I remember more about *not* eating in the hotel dining room where there were thick, parchmentlike menus. While I was singing I couldn't take my eyes off the glamorous chrome compotes draped with shrimp which everyone seemed to be eating. This isn't *Oliver Twist,* and we always had more and better, delicious Jewish home cooking. But to this day, to this very day, I get a stab in the heart, and a mini anxiety attack when I have to order from an imposing menu, no matter who's paying. My eyes go right away, hippity-hop to the price. I cannot order the most expensive dish, or a full-course dinner a la carte unless I am heavily sedated. Now, you have to know that I have eaten with royalty, and also show biz greats from Maxim's to Moscowitz and Lupowitz, and yet, whenever I manage to sneak a look at the check, or the American Express receipt, I feel a little guilty.

I didn't mean to go on. I really want to talk about cash. You know, now that I'm *so* grown up, when people ask me what I want as a present, I say, "Oh, nothing, oh, well, a good book, or a classical record would be lovely, thank you . . . Really you shouldn't . . . I have everything." What I really want to say is: "Cash . . . just give me the money, and I mean, if you throw in what the cab to the store would have cost, that would be a terrific little gift." I remember how great it felt when I got my first salary from the hotel. It was sixty dollars—in bills. I took it into the ladies' room (I was still in my South American costume), and I spread the money on the floor around me. The patrons walked in and out, but I didn't care. I looked at it, smelled it, touched it. I guess it must have been in ones, or maybe in the early forties paper money was bigger. But the picture in my mind is of little Phyllis and BIG bucks.

Soon I was playing all over New Jersey as Baby Phyllis Baker and having great success. Belle Baker was appearing at the Loew's State on Broadway and we all wanted me to be seen, but there was a law in New York City in the early forties called the Gary law which said that minors could be on the stage in speaking parts, but could not sing or dance. A group of people called the Gary Society were responsible for this, in response to abuses of child performers. I was furious because it kept me from going "big time" vaudeville in New York. Then somebody had an irresistible notion. Belle would do most of her act and just before her knockout closing—which had something to do with bringing our boys home from the war—she'd stop and confide to the audience:

"Ladies and gentlemen, just a little while ago I was sitting in my dressing room, getting ready to come out here, and there was a knock on the door. I said, 'Come in' . . . I thought it was my precious Bessie who's been zipping me into my gowns since before there were zippers. (Big audience laugh.) There in front of me was a little girl holding tightly to her pretty mommy's hand. I said, 'Darling, what do you want? Belle has to be onstage in a few minutes.' She told me what a fan of mine she was and how she wanted to grow up to be a singer just like me; I was very touched,

Me and my "auntie"—
Belle Baker.

ladies and gentlemen, and I was about to sign an autographed picture for her when she asked if she could sing for me. She said it would just take a minute of my time, and her daddy, who had just come back from fighting for us, ladies and gentlemen, was waiting outside. Well . . . you know, ladies and gentlemen, that Belle's just an old softie. I said, 'Sure, honey, come on in and sing, but it has to be fast. I don't want to keep my beautiful audience waiting!' I'm not going to say a word . . . but, ladies and gentlemen, that little girl is in the audience with her mommy and daddy. . . . Would you like to hear her? (A big *yeah!* from the audience.) Let's see if we can get her up onstage." (Entire audience applauds and looks around.)

I pretend to squirm in my seat until the spotlight picks me out and then, maybe one touch too much, I turn to my parents and give them a wide, slightly toothless grin, and bound down the aisle and up the few steps up to the big, big stage. The audience is surprised to see the lack of size of me. It makes them laugh, and they applaud more. The microphone is enormous. I nod to Belle. She unscrews it at the center and lowers it to my size. She bends down and says: "Tell all these lovely ladies and gentlemen your name, darling."

"Well, my real name is Phyllis Newman, but I call myself Phyllis (good pause) Baker, and I hope you don't mind?"

She gives me such a big wet songstress kiss. "What a question . . . huh? (She points to me, she points to the audience, they respond appropriately.) What are you going to sing for us, Little Miss . . . Baker?"

"If you don't mind, I'd like to sing 'Music, Maestro, Please' (her big-hit torch song). Oh . . . could I please borrow your handkerchief?" (Her trademark that she uses frequently to wipe away the real tears.)

She gives me her long, trailing scarf. I twirl it around my finger the way she always does, I turn and point to the conductor in the pit below: "If you please, Mr. Zwerling."

I then sing her very adult song, in a very adult voice with what seems to be a real understanding of the lyrics.

Years later one of my first TV appearances was on a live variety show from Florida Sea World. I sang "I've Grown Accustomed to Your Face" to a seal.

Did it throw me? Did it throw the seal? Not at all. Were we great? Of course. We recognized each other from the Steel Pier. The old girl or guy and I threw our flippers and arms around each other, and kissed the air on each side of our cheeks . . . mwah . . . mwah. Look how far we'd come. He by water, of course, but never mind, we made it. There we were, doing a double on national television. Can I tell you just one more time? There is no business like . . . Well, maybe there is.

THREE

Cookie Rott lived two houses away from me on the "Boulevard" in Jersey City when we were about seven years old. Cookie was German and Christian. I was Jewish and Jewish. It was during the war. We had matching fake white lamb coats trimmed in red wool and red-knit Dutch-girl hats that tied under the chin. We were best, best . . . until the day Cookie called me "Dirty Jew" and I called Cookie "Dirty Nazi." Then we were *almost* best, best, but we began to be on the lookout for new material.

It wasn't easy for me in those days to hang on to civilian friends. I had to play down all of my show business activities. I had to play down my mother's telling people's fortunes in my bedroom. Cookie knew. The kids right in the neighborhood knew. But they never talked about it in front of me. My friends could visit only on Wednesdays and Sundays when my mother was "off." That's when I started working on my "normal" act, and because I was such a good mimic and a good liar, I perfected it.

My mother—Rachel—had blond Veronica Lake, Joan Blondell hair, a full but not fat body, a broad face, longish sharp nose, and small dancing eyes. She favored "sexy" clothes. Deep V-necks with lots of "bubbies" showing. Strong colors, costume jewelry, and hanging earrings. She looked like Mrs. Forties Modern, free and loose. She didn't have a trace of an accent although she hadn't arrived in America from Russia/Poland until she was thirteen. She was the most moral, strict, old-fashioned mother of them all. She had a drink or two sometimes. Never more. No smoking, cursing, off-color stories in front of the children. Cook nourishing meals. Keep up a front, hand your husband the money under the table to pay the bills. Sit up with sick children, be loving and tender with them beyond measure. Laugh, tell them stories, endless stories before bedtime. Sing . . . the saddest, oldest tearjerker songs. Lie in bed with the little girl for hours in the dark. Tell her she's the prettiest, smartest, most talented, and has the best future of anyone she's ever "read." Momma knows, Momma knows. After all, doesn't she always have a "den" full of ladies every night waiting for a "reading"? Momma hides the crystal ball somewhere in the kids' room when it's not in use. I never look for it. I am learning to ignore distressing evidence.

Rachel's father had brought her to America from Russia/Poland his second or third trip over. He had brought some of his other children on earlier trips, settled them with relatives, and gone back. There were thirteen or fourteen children, and about half of them stayed in Europe for emotional or physical reasons. His wife never came. She was a butcher, and she was earning the money. He was the scholar; he had more time. Like everybody else in their tiny Jewish enclave, they wanted their children to have those golden opportunities America afforded. Rachel and her younger sister Libby went to live in Cleveland where an older sister named Gussie had settled. There wasn't much happening in the way of school except English classes. Rachel was the best, she was the only one who wound up without an accent. So my granny was a butcher. Now you know, that's only charming to you when you hit forty or so and it's the 1980s or so, otherwise bury it, lose it, or romance it up. I buried it. Rachel

My mother and father.

probably didn't bury it, she didn't have to. All her young friends were immigrants from equally high-toned surroundings.

On the other hand . . . I never heard this bit of folklore from Rachel. I only found out about it from Aunt Libby after she died. Granted, I had a "roots" problem. Beginnings never interested me until my recent unpleasantness—not my family's or anyone else's. *Now*. How does it feel *now*? How are we doing *now? Tomorrow?* Will I turn into June Allyson with Selena Royle and Lewis Stone for Mommy and Daddy? No? Then save the stories. I'll wait until the movies and books come out—and they did. Just substitute your mom and dad for the leading characters and you've got a heart-tugging immigrant background.

Rachel and Sig married young. She was just sixteen. He was two or three years older. Sig, Sigmund Arthur from Warsaw, looked as if he could be Danny from Ireland. He had dark straight hair, large, round brown, merry eyes, a fine-boned, delicate face, and a perfect, remember? pug nose. They were cute, cute all the way.

One assumes, doesn't one, that they struggled, made love, grew up fast. One knows that they tried different businesses, stores, and before I was born, moved from Cleveland to New York with two daughters, Shirley and Elaine, wound up in Jersey City and had a third, unplanned daughter, me, many years later.

Sig couldn't really get "located" in Cleveland. Ray's family drove him crazy. The people he came into contact with didn't understand him. They were small town, small minds. He needed a new start. He needed New York where the big-timers were, where they would recognize him as one of their own. In no time at all he'd be one of them. Those big shots—he knew more than all of them. He had ideas. This was America and he was no greenhorn. He'd show them.

Ray loved him so much. She hated to move, but his jealousy and the friction drove her crazy. Maybe it would be better for them, for the girls. Maybe his luck would change. Maybe he'd find his place. Maybe he'd become a mensch.

Sig had two much older sisters who lived in Jersey City. They hadn't been close. No one was too close to him. They helped out the young family a very little bit. With the money they scraped together from part-time work, and probably some loans, the best Sig and Rachel could afford was a makeshift apartment in a storefront. The store's big window was completely covered with pasted-on brown paper to keep out the light and the street. Some of the previous tenants had obviously attempted to cozy up the place. Assortments of cheap curtains, remnants of their futile labor, were tacked all over the papered window wall.

Mother, Shirley, Elaine, and me; grammar-school graduation day.

There was one main room of modest proportions, and another tiny one that must have been a storeroom. It still had rotting shelves and a toilet and sink. The light source was the ever-popular naked light bulb on a frayed cord hanging from the ceiling. And that was it. The aunts gave them a few pieces of cast-off furniture. My mother felt humiliated, not because it was shabby or poor, but because to her it wasn't "respectable." For many generations "How does it feel?" took second place to "How does it look?"

Sig talked his way into a few jobs, mostly as a salesman working on commission only. They usually ended in a cloud of anger and accusations. There seemed to be just as many jerks in Jersey as in Cleveland. My parents were living completely on borrowed money in a kind of poverty they had never experienced. Sig's nutty bravado turned into desperation and then into paralyzing despair.

I wish I knew what happened then . . . what did he say? . . . what did she do? . . . when was the idea planted? How did a shy young woman from "the other side" assume her new "persona," her new "profession"? How did my mother turn into a fortune-teller who would be the sole support of her family and then herself until the day she died? Surely, you'd think I could find out. Someone would tell me. Well, I haven't and they won't, and I don't even know if they know. Of all the dumb things to be ashamed of—of all the skeletons, family secrets—this one is treated like an unspeakable aberration. Everybody knew and pretended they didn't. She wanted it that way. Am I violating her by trying to figure it out? By wanting to turn her story into a show, a book, a character for me to play? What the hell am I doing? I can't even write "her." I guess I want her to inhabit me . . . I want her to come back. I sort of get what I got from him, but I could do with some insight into the constant seesaws of my attention, my heart, and my spirits.

My first memory is asking my mommy to pull out her big titty. I nursed until long after I spoke simple declarative sentences. Nice work if you can get it.

Now I'm going to shape up and stick to the story, with details and inevitabilities. I certainly don't want to legitimize the minute-and-a-half attention span we hear so much about. We persist, insisting on form, reason, explanations. We won't recognize the breaking up of emotional molecules brought on by fear, drugs, alcohol, fear, chemicals, fear, technology, daily reminders of cosmic inhumanity . . . and life's little "vicissitudes."

So life proceeded on the boulevard in Jersey City. Momma told fortunes, I sang and talked in the carriage pushed by one of my sisters, and later on the street, holding another of my sisters' hand. Nobody asked me to, that's just what I did. If I were my sisters I would have wanted to stuff a scarf into my always-in-motion baby's mouth. They were adolescents by the time I was born. And they must have been thrilled to take care of me while Momma was working. They often had to take me along when they went out with friends. But didn't *I* have the best time? I sang away merrily to my captive audience.

Daddy, oh, Daddy . . . what was he doing then? Well, that could have been when he organized the "Police Scouts of America," an organization of young boys with the same general aims, requirements, and program of the Boy Scouts of America. He could have been doing that or what I called the "secret thing."

There was a small, deep (for Jersey City) closet in the "den,"
which, as I've told you, was filled most of the time with Momma's
customers. (The den also had an impossible upright piano,
stacked with music, my arrangements, and my oldest sister's yellowed arias.) This closet was stuffed with business cards, photos,
and stationery. The first thing my father did when he got an
idea, and he got so many, was to print business cards, letter-
heads, and brochures. We'd sit around the small, tin-topped
table in our crowded kitchen overlooking the boulevard and
my father would tell us his latest idea. They were invariably
born out of anger. Anger at the system, the incompetency, but
mostly (oh, how I hate to remember this), but mostly anger at
rejection.

"Ray, I . . . you . . . tell me why, why should I work for those
momzers, those dopes, for commission, when I can have my own
company? They don't know anything, they're crooks. I generate
my own action. I'm the idea man . . . then they give me a lousy
ten percent. I found a little storefront on Garfield Avenue. It's a
great location. It's very cheap. Ray, the whole thing will come
to . . . "

"Sig, shah, shah, not in front of the kinder."

"All right, all right. Here's my card. How do you think it
looks?"

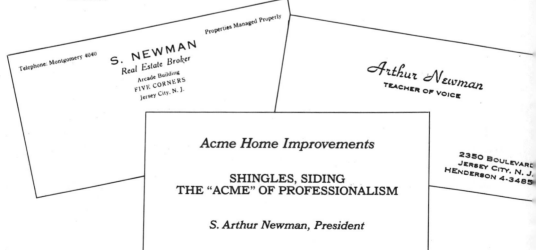

We knew Momma would give him the money. But we all had seen so many cards. We knew it would fail. We knew the game was in the setting-up, and the drudgery of the follow-through would defeat him. (Did we know it then? Or did we think . . . well, maybe? This does seem like a solid-looking business card.)

The "secret thing" was never mentioned by anyone. When I found the card in the closet, I didn't even ask my mother what it was. I didn't want her to get more embarrassed. And I certainly wouldn't ask my father; I didn't want him to get angry, or tell another fanciful, but always depressing, story.

This card was the simplest of all. No artwork, no catchphrases.

```
┌─────────────────────────────────────────┐
│                                         │
│                                         │
│                                         │
│         REVEREND ARTHUR NEWMAN          │
│               555-9246                  │
│                                         │
│                                         │
│                                         │
└─────────────────────────────────────────┘
```

What the hell was that all about? Many years later, I asked my mother and got a look that told me nothing.

Let's just go over here on the side . . . and amass a little daddy data. Slight, cute, angry, a great father, a nutso parent. More contradictions than a politician's concession speech. He drove the little kid from Jersey City to New York every day to the Professional Children's School. The kid would fake around the school with all the other young pros, half of whom had dyed red hair, because it was the time of *Life With Father* on Broadway. What did Daddy do? He hung out a lot in cafeterias with semi-Broadway cronies. He'd visit small- and medium-time agents getting work for the kid, and talking up his own latest scheme. (By now he was a hypnotist, a mentalist, and a trainer of "Puffy, the Hypnotizing Cat" who played Carnegie Hall to an audience of forty-five people—including my mother and me, heavily disguised.)

At two o'clock, whatever was *not* happening, he would get into his old dilapidated car of the moment and drive up to Broadway in the low Sixties and wait in front of the office building, two floors of which comprised this Professional Children's School.

I didn't appreciate it then; he drove me crazy. He used to say "Up and at 'em" at the start of each day's journey. Silly man. So how come, when this grown lady had to take her kids somewhere, especially when it's for a difficult destination, or maybe she's just feeling insecure about her kids, she had to stop herself from automatically saying, "Hey . . . up and at 'em"? And why is it when I had to get dressed to go to the hospital that first time, and my husband, my friend Bobbie, and I got downstairs and were about to hail a cab, and there was my sister Shirley, waiting in her Jersey car, waiting to take us over, driving nervously, speaking in a high-pitched and falsely cheerful voice, why did I, instead of saying a simple thank you to my sister, say, "Well, as Daddy used to say . . . Do you remember, Shirl? Up and at 'em"? Let me communicate with you, Shirley, and repair our often-broken connection, by showing you that he's in my heart, my soul. My strengths and weaknesses are his even though I tend to disparage him and you always stick up for him like Momma did.

Let me remind ourselves that when, at age eighteen, I went into a hospital for the first time ever, when the doctor found a small lump in my breast in Cleveland . . . that's right, the lump was in Cleveland. I came home and I had to go to the hospital where I was born to have it removed. All of this was rare, exotic, unknown in those early fifties days. Daddy just got into his bed and he couldn't move. I mean he *could not move* until the lump was out and I was out of the hospital and all right. The fear of losing me and his identification with my pain and terror paralyzed him. His golden baby in such terrible circumstances.

Daddy, Daddy, Daddy, I'm so glad you weren't here for this mess. "Remember, Shirl? 'Up and at 'em . . . Up and at 'em!' "

My mother took me to New York one day to a building in the Forties. We went up the elevator, down a long linoleum-covered corridor to a glass-paned door that had been newly lettered.

S. ARTHUR NEWMAN
HAND PAINTED HATS

We opened the door, my father was sitting on a folding chair. The "showroom" was a small, gray square space. The only decorations were a few standing wooden hat racks on which hung these mute felt shapes in various colors. I know my father had been staring straight ahead before we arrived. Isn't that just what I do—and maybe you, too—when the world is not enough with us? He jumped up when we came in and pulled his loose, small body together. He straightened his shoulders in another move, as he always did. He put on his smile by raising his high forehead until it made those little ridgy lines that took his eyebrows and eyes with them. His face was uneven—two different sides—and the smile only emphasized that. Every time I kissed him, I was surprised at how delicate and fragile and small-boned he felt, for someone who scared and upset me so much.

Then he took us on a tour of his hats. There were about twelve or fourteen. The first one was gray with a big off-the-face brim, on which was painted a clump of grapes in deep purple, with a little stem and everything. We said the grapes looked "almost" lifelike. And yes, Momma said, "Oh, they look so real I could take a bite out of them," and laughed. Then Daddy put the hat on Momma. It was too small for her large head. He put it on me and of course it was too big. But I modeled it and made a little funny, fast fashion show. I wanted to be excited and happy. Momma and I were doing our performance, our enthusiastic, normal, supportive, cheery . . . oh, you get the idea.

We stretched out clucking over the limited hat inventory . . . of red flowers on black . . . green leaves on the side of a brown cloche . . . until there was really nothing left for the three of us to do in that room. No phone rang, no one came in. We decided to go down to the coffee shop in the building.

Daddy closed and locked the door and took something out of his pocket that he stuck into the lower left-hand corner of the glass part of the door. It was a newly printed card that read:

BE BACK IN A MINUTE
OUT FOR COFFEE
S. ARTHUR NEWMAN

Good. Now the nonexistent customers knew exactly where they stood.

We visited him a few more times. My mother tried to drum up business, but it was difficult. As always, where my father succeeded was in getting publicity or some famous person involved. I don't know how, I guess that's what he really put his attention to. He missed his proper life slot. He should have been an entrepreneur—a producer—like Mike Todd. The last time I went there, before the inevitable fold, the place was the same, the hats remained unsold, and the only thing different was that there was a whole wall—*a whole wall*—of black-framed photos of my father and semifamous or nonfamous ladies wearing or holding the hats. But, by God, there was a picture of Lena Horne with her beautiful hands holding one side of a cherry-painted hat and my father holding the other side. He was looking at her and smiling that smile with those overly animated eyes, expectant, knowing this time it really was the start of something big.

I didn't actually start school until I was almost eight. Before Professional Children's School I had gone to what was called the "demonstration school" at State Teacher's College in Jersey City. I think it was called that because it was for the slightly gifted. I had to take a test to get in. I passed and was put into the second grade. I fooled around there for a few weeks and was quickly skipped into the third grade. I made a lot of new friends, but I had to keep on my toes. Don't forget, I had to do the major cover story about my mother and her "work" and my father and his lack of it.

I was naturally bright, I read like a bandit, and what I didn't know I made up. Once we had a class assignment to bring in information about Jersey City's services and how they were run. It was to be a verbal report from everyone in the class. As my classmates droned on about the waterworks, the police department, the hospital system, my panic accelerated. I was unprepared but sure I could improvise my way through something, give them a laugh, and sit down. But those little goody-goodys had facts and figures and cunning little charts. I wanted to swat them, and I wanted to show them.

"Garbage . . . my subject is garbage. My uncle . . . Joe is a garbageman and he drives one of those big garbage trucks." (My room at home was on the first floor and faced a side street alley, where the garbage was set out in large tin cans and picked up every day. I would listen for it and stare out at those beefy guys and I guess it left more of an impression than I realized.) "When I got this assignment I asked Uncle . . . Joe if I could ride on the truck with him and see firsthand a day in the life of . . . garbage. We drove around and he and his two assistants Mike and Sal, they drove on the back of the truck. They picked up hundreds of heavy cans and dumped the garbage in the truck. They have a hard job. It was really interesting . . . thank you."

I sat down fast, but not fast enough.

"That's a very unusual report, Phyllis. Tell us what happens to the garbage at the end of their run. How do we dispose of our waste in Jersey City?"

I answered without a second's hesitation.

"They drove the truck down to the water and they dumped all the garbage into the ocean."

I sat down again, satisfied. Some kids were whispering, a few were laughing. I didn't know why.

"They dumped the garbage right into the ocean? That's a long way to go. We live on the river that runs into the ocean. You're sure they dumped the garbage into the water . . . just like that?"

I knew I had really stepped in it, but I had no way out but to stick to my story. She wouldn't dare call me a liar, she'd just think I was disturbed.

"That's just the way it happened . . . and if you don't believe me, call my uncle Joe."

"Fine . . . thank you. Next Janet will report on nurses."

It was never mentioned again, and I still don't really know where garbage heaven is.

I guess I ran out of fascinating fake relatives who worked for the city, because a couple of years later I changed schools and started three years of almost perfect nonattendance at the Professional Children's School in New York City. The school was founded to provide an education for children who were working in the performing arts. It catered to their special needs by offering weekly assignments in all subjects that you could do by correspondence, if your work interfered with school hours. You could come back at any time and have kept up with the rest of your class, because (theoretically) everyone was doing the same thing at the same time. You were supposed to send in your written work every week, and do the assigned reading. For a while, Daddy drove me there every day and I really loved it. Then I simply stopped going in person and I don't know why. I was working some club dates, occasional vaudeville and auditioning. But I don't remember anything so pressing that would have prevented me from going, or from doing any homework. I simply lied to everyone. I told my parents I had mailed it in. I told the school that it must have been lost.

How did I get away with it? I went in every so often and took all the tests. I crammed and passed everything. My excuses were fanciful, my style, when I spoke to my judges, was direct, humble and honest. I guess I was a real actress. Or is it possible that I fooled no one?

At the end of the seventh grade I told my parents that I really wanted to go back to "regular school" in Jersey City. We lived three blocks away from the cutoff street for P.S. 17. That was the school I wanted, because many of my friends were there. It was in the "good neighborhood." I gave the address of one of my mother's "ladies"—Mrs. M. Mrs. M. and her daughter were our only crossover friends. They were rich by our standards, and part of the fabulous Jersey City Jewish "society." She was a big client of Momma's and her daughter was one of the tight circle of six girls of which I was determined to be part.

That meant that both of them had to keep their mouths closed about us, at least within earshot. Who did we think we were kidding? Why did we work at it so hard? Why did I lust—and I mean lust—after those girls' parents, their apartments, their clothes, their food, their bedrooms, their confidence, their security, their futures?

During that period—the twelve-to-fifteen-year-old syndrome —I wanted only one thing . . . to be them. All right, I wanted two things—them and boys. The boys part was easy, but I never did get to be "them."

A lot of things came together for me in eighth grade at P.S. 17, including my hormones. I resolved to start building a proper life as had been told me and shown me in the movies. I thinned down and flirted up. I threw myself into studies, and was appalled at the gaps in my education. When the teachers spoke about history, pronouns, algebra, even home economics, it was as if they were speaking in tongues. All those years of nonattendance had paid off. I was ignorant. So I applied myself, as they used to say. I also applied makeup and my first bras and first stockings. I majored in crushes. I was not allowed to have a date with a boy, so there was a lot of schoolyard-concrete hanging around. No touching, absolutely no touching. I was too scared of my parents. I graduated with very respectable grades, the promise of a boyfriend, and . . . I became a temporary full-fledged member of the six and sometimes even the four, which was too select even to contemplate.

I'll just give you the straight facts about high school, and somehow we'll muddle through the psychological piece of the jigsaw puzzle it's supplying. What do you say?

Student's Name . . . Phyllis Newman

Address . . . 2350 Hudson Boulevard, Jersey City

Father's Occupation . . . Building contractor and dreamer

Mother's Occupation . . . Housewife and flourishing fortune-teller (for unofficial eyes only)

Grades . . . Well above average

Physical Characteristics . . . Well above average, long dark hair, lively and overanimated

Extracurricular Activities . . . cocaptain of the cheerleaders, lead roles in many school plays, chorus, works on yearbook, voted class leader most likely to succeed, and teacher's pet

Social Life . . . Terribly busy, has boyfriend who's a looker from rival school where he's captain of baseball and basketball team and president of class. They "go steady." They also go to the movies every single Saturday night. They never go out with any other friends. He's Catholic and blond and hates show business.

Summary . . . Phyllis is having one hell of a swell time. She's Betty coed, she's got the pre–Doris Day syndrome, you can't detect her previous life on her anywhere. She's destined to become a secretary and then a wife and mother.

There you sort of have it. My boyfriend went to Columbia University to study predentistry and I didn't have a clue as to what I wanted, except to see him and to get him.

The rest of our girls' group went off to college too. I guess I was lost, but I didn't know it. I was consumed with the guy. The only reason I got a job was that it brought me to New York City where he was, and gave me enough money to buy some clothes and pay my transportation. My first job was at B. Altman's department store. I started out as a stock girl and wound up selling children's clothes. I loved it. The aisles, the glass display cases, the piles of small T-shirts, pajamas, the little dresses hung up became my world. I was conscientious, I made the crusty older women, "who'd been there since . . ." laugh. I had no other ambition. I wanted to stay there forever if only the guy would marry me. After Christmas, perfect though I was, they laid me off. I felt betrayed. My social life consisted of going up to Columbia whenever he'd ask me, which was not too often, and seeing him for our weekly Saturday night movie in Jersey City. He came home most weekends. I was filled with jealousy for the unnamed and unseen—by me—masses of gorgeous blond coeds I was convinced he cottoned to every second. My obsession with him informed the next few years of my life in a very deep and not terribly healthy way. From the song "You may call it madness, but I call it Love."

I spent the rest of that first year out of school working as a file clerk. Then I was promoted to junior secretary in the New York City office of Burlington Mills. As long as I was close to the guy, I felt I probably had put all the exotica of show business and my unconventional parents behind me and was well on the way to respectability. Now he'd *have to want to marry me* . . . and at last I could turn into my perception of an uncomplicated, devoted girlfriend, wife, and mother of the fifties.

My parents were very angry with me. They felt I was wasting my time and my talent on an unresponsive, uncommunicative, rather testy young man. They were right. I was still living at home and we didn't get along. I wanted to be loyal to them and to him. I needed to get out. Somehow we decided just a couple of weeks before the fall term started that I would, a year after graduation, try to get into college. They wanted me to be away from him. I wanted to be away from them. I took a test and was accepted into Flora Stone Mather College of Western Reserve University in Cleveland. It made sense, right? I had other family there, and it was a good school. And it was movement.

Do you have to be told by now that I fit right in? That I loved my roommate from Sandusky, Ohio? That I had a nice Cleveland semiboyfriend who adored me? That I did well? Even so, whenever I could, I put notices up on the bulletin board or answered ones for rides to New York. The car rides took twelve, fourteen, who knows how many, all-night hours. I would go right up to Columbia and be with the guy. He didn't beg me to, but I did.

It involved elaborate cover stories for my parents. I did them well, they never found out. On one trip home, an official one, when I was staying in Jersey City, I saw an item in the theater pages about an open audition for a new musical called *Wish You Were Here*. They wanted young people who could sing and swim, there was going to be a real swimming pool onstage. I hadn't even finished the second term of my first year at college, but I was anxious to be closer to the boyfriend again.

I didn't let the fact that I couldn't swim stop me. I took a strapless navy bathing suit and a piece of sheet music in a brown paper bag. When I got to the Imperial Theatre, there was a line of young men and women hopefuls that went all around the block. I waited, they saw us twenty at a time, they typed us out. That means they decided who looked possible even before we sang, and thanked the rest. You've all seen *A Chorus Line*, right? So they get to me, they ask me to come back the following day to sing and/or read and I tell them—them being Joshua Logan, Leland Hayward, and Harold Rome—"I'm sorry, but I have to get back to college if I don't get this part." They laugh. Mr. Logan says, "All right, why don't you sing for us right now?" I do. I get the part. I go back to Cleveland only to get my duds and Betty Coed becomes Chiquita Chorine.

I came out of my six-year self-imposed retirement. The show was about summer romance among young singles in a Catskill-like hotel. The cast was unusually young, fresh, and inexperienced. We had endless rehearsals even after we opened. The show got terrible reviews but Mr. Logan and Leland Hayward, the producer, believed it would find an audience if they made some changes. They brought in Jerome Robbins to do a new dance, other people to do additional work, and the show had a good long run. I was chosen to understudy the female comic dancing lead. I wasn't a trained dancer, but I worked hard and fearlessly and got to play the role and do the complicated, difficult dances during the star's vacation.

The guy didn't hang around the theater a lot at all. He was kind of grumpy about the whole thing. I started going to Columbia U. College of Fine Arts during the day. Guess why?

So this was the picture: I still lived in Jersey City on the boulevard. I would come into New York by bus and subway up to Columbia, take a few classes and try to see him. Often, I would have a lot of time to kill. The library up there became my way station. Now I realize how lucky I was to be obsessed with a student at a great college. I took an interesting acting class with, among others, Tony Perkins. I studied European literature with an inspired, vital professor. Then I would go downtown to our communal chorine dressing room, do the show, walk to the station, take a bus home to Jersey City, where my father would be sitting at the lighted kitchen window watching for me. I'd wave to him from across the street when I got off the bus, and he'd open the window if necessary so that he would be able to see me until I reached the courtyard at the front of our apartment building. Then he would run to the front door (we were on the first floor), hold it open for me and make sure that I had made it all right. What an embarrassment, I thought then . . . What a daddy, I think now.

And the guy? Oh, the guy stayed a neurotic attachment through trips to Hollywood, through other guys. There was no logic, no reality and unfortunately little joy. The O. Henry touch is that he abandoned dental school, I got him his first job as a— here it comes—theatrical agent. He was and is incredibly successful at it. And yes, he was my agent for a part of my life. He's happy, a father, a husband, and weren't we both lucky?

Although my emotional life was on hold, my career kept moving. I did a number of The Golden Age of Live Television shows, among them "Studio One," "Philco Television Playhouse," "Kraft Television Theatre," "Robert Montgomery Presents," and others. It was, indeed, a golden time for a young actress. I played a variety of roles directed by some of the best. It was at one of these shows that I met and was hired by the director Sidney Lumet, who has remained part of my extended family.

During these years as I was working, studying, and trying to grow as an actress and musical performer, I had one close Jersey City friend whose interests and desires were running parallel to mine. Jerry Herman and I met as young children. His beautiful mother and mine, his proud father and mine, all felt that they and we were handpicked. He wrote a musical for the Jewish Community Center, when we were just pre- or newly teens. It was called *Step Right Up*, and it was set in a circus. We still sing the songs, which reach you the way all of Jerry's songs do. I was the lead. We were pleased with the show and with each other. I would often take the bus with him during our real teen years, typing up the lyrics on a portable typewriter on the way to New York. In the city I'd sing his songs for prospective anybodys. We were the real McCoy Mickey and Judy. We shared then, and still

My "making the rounds" picture.

do, an appreciation bordering on hysteria of certain American songs and singers. We were among the number one nut brigade of Judy Garland fans. We can still sing not only her vocal line, but almost every instrument's line of her arrangements. Once we drove down to Philadelphia when she was appearing at a theater there. We waited in the alley by the stage door for her to come out. After about an hour, we saw that the light was still on in what we assumed to be her dressing room. We were desperate, because we had to get back to Jersey City that night. So we started singing her arrangements, her songs, until she looked out the window, laughed, and waved to us.

We were not children, we were quite grown up when this particular folly was acted out. We dreamed of really belonging to the world of the musical theater. If this is getting just too cute and cloying . . . if the gee whiz of it is taking away your appetite, you have but just to say "knock it off, lady" and I certainly will not tell you about the opening night of Jerry's *Hello, Dolly!* when we looked at each other, hugged, and remembered. And I absolutely will not tell you how with each high- or low light of each other's work, we connect, we are grateful, and we still feel like kids.

As we started inching toward our dreams, we continued to enthuse about and stay involved with each other's work. In the mid-fifties Jerry wrote a revue called *I Feel Wonderful,* which was optioned for the Theatre De Lys in Greenwich Village. It was a funny, imaginative show and I was one of the small, varied but close-knit cast. One night we heard that Warner Brothers director Michael Curtiz was going to be in the audience, and that he was casting a new film version of the operetta *The Vagabond King* by Rudolf Friml. It was an intimate theater and Curtiz was an imposing figure with an imposing retinue. We sparkled plenty, and told each other how we were sure that he would just love *them.* We were all desperate to be discovered for the movies.

After the show, the stage manager told us to hurry back down to the stage from our narrow, shared section of the fly-space-divided-by-a-curtain dressing room. *He* was so impressed that *He* was coming backstage. *He* was a tall, distinguished, rather attractive, shifty-looking Hungarian. He behaved the way you dreamed a Hollywood director would. He had a thick accent and his gestures were flamboyant. He wore a floor-grazing camel's hair coat on his shoulders, for God's sake. The coat did not have a belt just across the back, but all the way around and hung loosely through its loops.

He told us, "My darlings . . . darling little people . . . little actors . . . little geniuses . . . brilliant . . . simply brilliant." And then he kissed each one of us, and his coat never slipped from his shoulders. The next day we were called by the casting director to read for the picture. All the girls were reading for Huguette, the soubrette.

That night at the theater we compared notes. The describing of auditions to other actors is almost always done with caution. You don't want to sound self-satisfied, or too hard on yourself . . . but you *do* want to slip in the fact that they *adored* you. After we had one round of this, one of the girls shyly told us that after her reading she looked up and Mr. Curtiz was openly weeping. He took her hands in his and said, "My Huguette . . . my perfect little Huguette" . . . as the casting director stared straight ahead. Another one of the girls looked stricken and told us that the exact same thing happened to her. One by one we all admitted that we had had the same scene word for word and tear for tear. We laughed, but none of us really found it very funny. We all secretly felt that we had gotten the part. Well, we were all hired, none of us to play Huguette. She was played by Rita Moreno.

It was a once in a lifetime thrill . . . my first part in a movie to be made in Hollywood—the Hollywood before television, the California that a young New Jersey–based New York actress had never seen. Never mind that we were really used as chorus people. Never mind that if you see the movie today (and there's little chance of that, it was a floperoo that was cut down to about an hour and released exclusively in garages in Nome, Alaska), you will be hard pressed to see my full face. You'll see a slice of my nose or chin and hear my one line that I must say I do awfully well. Our hero, played by a Maltese tenor named Oreste Kirkop, swivels his ample body toward me and I exclaim, "You haven't forgotten your Lulu, have you?"

In Los Angeles I was rooming with one of the dancers from New York. She was a lively, adorable, dark, curly-haired muscular girl. She looked like a young Greek boy. We got along very well in a comfortable one-bedroom apartment that the studio had found for us. We both met guys, and had dates, but I suspected that she was more sophisticated than I about men . . . oh, hell . . . what a thing . . . I've told you my most profound feelings. I've bared my physical truth and here I am pussyfooting about telling you that I was, what was called then, a good girl . . . a *virgin*. There it is. It's out. The real shame of the cities, the revelation that's going to put this book right over the top, memoir-wise.

My roommate was "dating" one of the makeup men on our picture. One night he was coming over to visit her and I was supposed to be out. My plans fell through and I was there when he arrived. The three of us had some food, and then the makeup man started telling us about the masks he made of the stars. We were fascinated. He asked me if I'd like to have one. He said that he had the plaster with him to make the cast. Before I had much of a chance to decide, I was sitting in the small kitchen on a wooden chair near the sink and he was putting some oil on my face and then putting a grayish whitish chalky paste on my face and straws into my nostrils so that I could breathe.

In the fifties, I had
some teeny tiny parts
in movies.

Let's Rock with Julius
LaRosa

Susan Strasberg (*to my
left*) and Kim Novak (*second from right*), on the set
of the movie *Picnic*,
which was directed by
Joshua Logan (*top*).

Here I am between Nick Adams (*left*) and William Holden (*right*) in
Picnic.

"But . . . but . . . " Mouth sealed shut, thank you.

I sat there with this stuff hardening. I couldn't move. I had to hold my head against the back of the chair for fear of dislodging the straws which were the only two things between me and asphyxiation. I have no idea how long I sat like that. I stopped counting at three million six. Finally they came back and he pried, and I mean pried, this plaster off my face. He then gently rubbed more oil on my skin to take off the remaining bits of hardened plaster and told me not to look in a mirror for a while as the redness might jar me and anyway it would be gone in a few hours.

When I could focus my eyes again, I saw that they both looked a little more relaxed and warmer toward me. Well, even a virgin has brains and feelings, and I realized that I had been had. But not as excitingly as my roomie. I've lost track of her. I know that she didn't see much of the makeup man after that. I was never angry with her, it was just too ingenious a way to get rid of me, and anyway I still have a plaster mask of my face complete with wire across the back suitable for hanging.

FOUR

I met Adolph when I auditioned to be Judy Holliday's standby in *Bells Are Ringing*. I almost didn't make it. I was and still am horrified by auditions. I find every reason not to go. If I do show up, I dress wrong, my nerves turn me into some other person, sometimes a wimp, bowing and scraping and trying to please, sometimes tough and brassy like Ethel Merman's untalented second cousin. Well, this time I got to the stage door and panicked and left. I knew Jule Styne and Betty Comden and Adolph Green, the Broadway biggies, were there. I was in my early twenties and Judy Holliday was an older great star. No way, I had decided. Besides there was this cheery, inviting coffee shop right down the street where I could get a BLT and a Coke. No contest, right? A woman who was sort of managing me at the time had set up this audition. When I didn't arrive on time, she came looking for me. She knew my pattern by now. She told me I was crazy to blow the opportunity to be seen by this group. She talked me into going back.

Well, you've seen enough movies to know how truly depressing theater auditions are. The stage is usually dark except for a

From left, Sydney Chaplin, Judy Holliday, and Adolph.

naked bulb on a stand that's called a work light. The people who are auditioning you are the unlit audience. The "Very nice, thank you" which means "Good-bye, Charlie" is usually said from the dark. It's when you start to see actual features of actual faces making their way down the blackened aisle that your heart soars . . . momentarily. At least you have made enough of an impression for them to show themselves. I saw a small, boyish face and figure bouncing down the aisle, talking all the way.

"Jesus, that was great, darling . . . of course, you're too young and pretty . . . she'll kill us . . . I'd like you to try it up a tone . . . darling, this is a big theater to fill."

I sang a few bars, up a tone.

"O.K., O.K., good . . . now, darling, let's push it up one more tone, and when you come to the C sing it full out . . . I want you to reach the balcony."

I wasn't completely sure which note the C was, but I planted my feet firmly on the quicksand, and sang to Mr. and Mrs. Balcony.

He looked both happy and worried at the same time.

"Betty, Adolph, do you want to hear her read?"

"Sure, Jule."

And then in chorus, "Have her read the wake-up scene."

I read the scene, a funny, charming first in-person meeting of the hero and heroine. (She's an answering-service operator who's been meddling in his life on the phone using an old lady's voice. They have never seen each other. Now it would have to be a machine that comes to his house, but never mind.)

I read with the stage manager. It was a long scene, and they didn't interrupt. I was really getting into the character of Ella Peterson, and I forgot my nerves. I was sorry when it ended. This time three whole faces came out of the Twilight Zone: Jule; an attractive, businesslike woman; and an elf in black leather pants, chewing a cigarette. They were all really excited. They complimented me sincerely and indicated I'd gotten the job.

Being Judy Holliday's standby was thrilling, frustrating, glamorous, and tedious. My job was to be at the theater a half hour before curtain time, and to be sure that Judy was able to play. She was . . . for all but three performances in the year or so I was with the show. I was supposed to stay around until the beginning of the second act in case something happened. I was able, after a while, to leave, or call in, as long as I left a number where I could be reached quickly if necessary. It's funny, I just realized that I still have recurring anxiety dreams about not leaving my number or being unavailable when the theater calls.

I was so smitten with the theater that it was no chore to watch Judy, Sydney Chaplin, Jean Stapleton, and the rest of that talented cast perform night after night. Most times I'd watch part of the show. There were certain logistic problems. I had no place of my own, no dressing room, not even in the "Ladies Ensemble" room, which was in the basement. It was a big space with many mirrors and chairs lined up along the sides. But every mirror was taken. Michelle, who sat on one end, next to the curtain that separated the "dressing room" from the "wardrobe room," let me pull up a chair next to her and hang around. She was a tall blonde with a great voice and a dry delivery of observant humor. The chorus room was the two-way filter of company gossip, and there was always plenty. Judy and Sydney had been an item,

inseparable during rehearsals, out of town, and for a long time
after the opening. Then something happened, and now they
didn't even speak offstage. Lines were drawn. Sydney didn't care
if you were friendly with Judy, but Judy had to have utter loyalty. So the cast had to do fancy footwork, because most of us
were crazy about both of them.

Sydney was matinee-idol handsome, sweet, emotionally remote in the usual ways, but very much present with his outrageous sense of the absurd. He made fun of everything: sex,
religion, politics, and bodily functions. He was so quick, so im-
provisatory, so far out, and totally without malice that he of-
fended no one. It was insane nonsense with truth at its center.

Adolph was, and is, smallish, slender, dark-skinned with a
funny nose and teeth that have a life and story of their own. He
doesn't really resemble anyone else. He always looks suspicious
and guilty, as though he has just done something he shouldn't
have. He rarely looks you straight in the eye. He seems to be
hiding something, but I've never found out what it is. Is it all
just because he's Hungarian?

Adolph began his career in the thirties as a poor, uncastable,
eccentric actor. He met Judy Holliday, who was then really working as a switchboard operator, Betty Comden, and two young
actors, Alvin Hammer and John Frank. They devised an act
called The Revuers and did it for little pay at Max Gordon's
Village Vanguard. They wrote their own material because they
couldn't afford writers. Once in a while their pal Leonard Bernstein would play, but mostly he was an appreciative audience.
They were witty, bright, and original. They started building a
reputation and attracting a heady audience of people in both
the entertainment and intellectual worlds. Adolph and I have
compared early vaudeville experience and it's possible, just possible, that we once played the same theater at the same time with
Mildred Bailey and Henny Youngman. A sobering thought. He
said that they usually bombed in commercial houses. I don't
remember, but if it happened, I was pre-pre-puberty and he was
post-anything worth mentioning.

Adolph was around the theater a lot because he was a close
friend of both Judy and Sydney. I was attracted to him, but I

was intimidated by his age, his reputation as an intellectual, his success, and, most of all, by his mind-boggling eccentricity. Nevertheless, I took to sitting on the back steps, where he was bound to see me when he came in the stage door. I also took to reading a higher class of book. Don't get me wrong, I had read all kinds of books up until then. I just got a little more selective to impress the current market. I replaced Jacqueline Susann with Jane Austen, and Irving Wallace with Wallace Stevens. He started paying attention to me and I was flattered. I took stock of the situation and realized that all of his friends and colleagues were (A) older and smarter than I was, (B) more sophisticated and successful than I was, (C) better dressed than I was, and (D) I'd bullshit my way through!

He finally asked me out for a real date and I would have freaked, but that expression wasn't around then. He took me to Sardi's, "The Showman's Paradise," as he called it. The hot seats there are the banquettes along the wall to the left as you come in. They seated us at hot table #2. Right next to us were Ruth Gordon and Garson Kanin. On the wall just above us was a caricature of Alfred Lunt and Lynn Fontanne. I started fantasizing what a fabulous show biz/intellectual couple we could be. I had rehearsed our entire conversation in my head the night before—both parts—but it wasn't happening. I was really feeling ill at ease. When the waiter came over, I said, "I'll have a Scotch on the rocks . . . with ice, please." Then I turned to Adolph and said, "This is so exciting . . . it makes me think of the opening paragraph of *The Case of Sergeant Grischa* by Arnold Zweig. But for sheer, attentuated length . . . you just can't beat those sentences of Marcel Proust." I tried to laugh, world-weary-like. He tried to make believe that I was making sense. I felt like a fraud, a fool, and a cliché. I wasn't any of those things, but that's how I was behaving.

Somehow, I got through the evening. I don't quite know how to characterize it as first dates go. Terror: ten. Sparks: three and a half. Interest: seven. I guess he was bemused but not really thrilled with me either. I haven't asked him about it yet. I'm waiting for our fiftieth anniversary to sit the man down and have a real talk. I only know he didn't ask me out for a very long time after that date.

I wasn't completely left to languish on the stairs. I still had my old "guy," and some nights I'd go out with Sydney Chaplin and other members of the cast. Their hangout was Goldie's, a cozy East Side *boîte*, where Goldie Hawkins and Wayne Sanders played great two-piano arrangements of popular and show tunes. It was a sophisticated after-theater, late-night bar and restaurant. It was in the basement of a town house, down a few steps, dimly lit and very narrow. A lot of space was taken up by the two pianos and the bar. There were a few tables and it had a great huddly feeling.

One night I was there with Sydney, Michelle (my dressing room buddy) and their friend Gene Kelly. Yes, Gene Kelly. We were sitting around; they were drinking and singing along with the pianos. I was staring and pinching myself and enjoying it and laughing at Sydney and then—in the best tradition of the movies of the time—Fred Astaire walked in, shoulders leading, head slightly forward, springy. Just like we've all seen him walk in all our lives.

There was no time for awe or awkwardness. As soon as Sydney spotted him, he said in his loud, hoarse, laugh-filled voice: "Jesus Christ! If it isn't the other old hoofer himself! By God, I took these two guys out of the gutter, worked with them on their fucking arabesques till I got a hernia, and do they ever thank me? Nooo. Do they ask me to do my famous beached-whale imitation in their movies? Nooo . . . "

Astaire and everybody else is laughing. Sydney throws his bear arms around him.

"Hey, Fred, how are you, buddy?" (Remember to see and hear the completely charming, devilish merriment in Sydney's eyes and voice.)

Astaire and Kelly hug. I hug myself because I'm there. Sydney makes the sweetest introductions all around. Astaire sits down. There is no tension or pomposity because of Sydney. Goldie and Wayne start playing songs vaguely connected to the two of them. I mean no one had the gall to play "Singin' in the Rain" or

"Easter Parade." I mean this was sophisticated New York City—
a little easy Gershwin, some humming, some laughing, a drink
or two, some trading off of half choruses. And then the two of
them got up and started dancing improvisatorily around the tiny
available spaces, using people, chairs, the pianos, and the bar as
props for invention and limitations. They were as stunning
dancing spontaneously as they were in their carefully worked
out film numbers.

That year, when I was in the show and while Adolph and I
were reconnoitering each other, his universe of accomplished
and recognized people was becoming highly seductive. They
were his colleagues, friends, mentors. I'm still seduced. I'm still
a superfan of people with talent, intellect, originality. My face
becomes very alive and my body sings when I'm with these life-
enhancing, oddball, driven, successful figures.

> *Call me superficial.*
> *Call me Ishmael.*
> *Call me starstruck or leave me alone, which is even better.*

I've always had many friends of my own, especially women
friends, the same ones for a long time. We were supportive of
each other even before we knew what that word meant. I want
you to know some of the ones who got me through the tough
times. You've met Felicia, you know Lauren Bacall, of course,
but not my girlfriend Betty Bacall, even if you've read her wonderful book.

One night Adolph came to fetch me after the show accompanied by Betty B. It was early on in our courtship. I was
knocked out, as everyone is, by her presence and her beauty.
She was an old friend of Adolph's and they acted then, as they
still do, like loving, bickering relatives. She and I hit it right on
because we're each what used to be called a woman's woman.
Her frontal attack on sham and dishonesty is well documented.
Together, we've done many of the things real girlfriends do.
We've sat with our babies in the park, we've commiserated over
lost-and-found or wandering loves, we've taken several non-
public, nontheatrical European trips alone together which we

dubbed "Our hearts were middle-aged and gay." She's made fun of my lack of housekeeping skills and my nongreen thumb. She is a perfectionist, and her house, her garden, and most of all her friendships reflect that.

No one became or remained my authentic, close friend because of their celebrity, but their talent stimulated and nourished me and being around so much of it possibly confused me.

Adolph courted me warily, taking me out from time to time and then from time to time to time. I didn't think of him very seriously. He was too old, too previously married, and too eccentric. Yet I liked him a lot.

I've had only two proper, well, hardly proper, but permanent homes in my life: with my parents and with Adolph. In the intervening years, the ones I'm telling you about now, I lived sometimes in a terrible hotel in the West Fifties, never quite unpacked, or on a couch in the apartment of two girls I barely knew, and for a while in an East Side luxury building where I had one small room overlooking a wall. The gas wasn't turned on in the Pullman kitchen hidden by folding doors, and I certainly didn't bother to do it. I didn't drink coffee and I only ate take-out sandwiches and potato chips when I was home. I had a TV set that someone had thrown out. The antenna had snapped off, but I put a wire hanger in the hole where the antenna had been. If I jiggled it, it sometimes connected and then it was good for hours of snow, occasionally interrupted by a picture. But I was never home anyway. Of course, the apartment had no furniture—no problem. But no bed—problem. My friend Ruth Dubonnet, who was then Jule Styne's "friend," had an extra Empire settee. Do you know what they look like? I didn't then, but after sleeping on it for months, I could draw it in the dark. It is a very-low-to-the-floor, wood-framed thing with curved arms; the left arm is much higher than the right, but in this case, it could be unhooked and folded down so that it became an extension of the seat so you could put your feet on it. Oh, damn. Do you know the picture of Madame Récamier in her Empire gown and curls, leaning on one arm and feet up in front?

By then I had left *Bells Are Ringing,* and gone on to get the part of Jane, the "pretty one," in a musical version of *Pride and*

Prejudice called *First Impressions.* Adolph and I were still dancing around each other. He'd come to visit me in Philadelphia where we were trying out the show before its Broadway opening. Abe Burrows was the director and adapter. Jule Styne was the producer. At the same time, Jule was in the middle of writing the score for *Gypsy* with Steve Sondheim. Since we had gotten bad reviews, Jule would sometimes come down for the night to cheer us up. We were putting in new scenes and new songs every night, rehearsing every day, and generally going nuts trying to make it work.

Let me set the scene. We're in Abe Burrows's hotel suite after the show. Abe thinks like Immanuel Kant, but talks like Casey Stengel. The composer and lyricist are looking pale, exhausted but eager for suggestions. It's their first show and it's a toughie. It's dying out there every night. Abe, the brilliant veteran of *Guys and Dolls,* is losing his perspective. The show was based on

First Impressions with Hermione Gingold (*left front*) and Polly Bergen (*right front*).

a delicate, subtle English masterpiece that had to be made enter-
taining for an American audience but still retain some spirit of
the original work. The cast is large and talented, with a variety
of styles and accents. Hermione Gingold plays Mrs. Bennet, the
mother of five marriageable daughters. She is English, God
knows, and enormously skilled, but her strength and eccentricity
seem to make her character dominate the story. Polly Bergen
plays Elizabeth Bennet, the headstrong and smart eldest daughter. Her tempestuous romance with the elegant Mr. Darcy is the
central thread (listen, guys, this is better than Classic Comics).
Polly is beautiful, a hell of a singer and actress, very famous and
popular, and very American. Her fans who come to see her in
the show are frustrated to see and hear her hemmed in by the
restraints of the character. So we're all crowded into this room,
looking to Jule Styne, our producer and our creative force,
to bail us all out. Jule sits down at the piano. Is it an idea for a
new song for Polly? He plays a few notes. They're gorgeous. He
says:

> "I tell you, Steve Sondheim brought in this lyric yesterday. I fell
> down! Fell . . . fucking down! He's a fucking genius. Listen to this.
> The kid is left alone. It's her birthday. She's got this stuffed animal.
> (He starts playing rapturously and reverently and then starts sing-
> ing at the top of his loud lungs.) "Little La-aa-mb . . . Little
> La-aa-mb . . . I wonder how old I am?!"

Jule is singing and playing for this captive audience the entire
score of *Gypsy* like a composer possessed. We, who have to face
yet another indifferent audience in just a few hours, are speech-
less. Abe tries to interrupt.

"Gorgeous, Jule, gorgeous. Now, what if we give Polly . . . "

"Yeah, yeah, great great idea . . . So, now Rose is trying to con
this guy . . . and she sings . . . 'Have an egg roll, Mr. Goldstone . . . ' I mean, is that a line? Is that a song line? *Have an egg
roll, Mr. Goldstone!* You see? She's so excited to have this producer, and . . . "

Abe again: "Yeah, great, Jule, great, but you're here for only one night. We gotta fix this show. Polly ain't landing. The songs ain't landing. Only the fucking scenery is landing . . . "

Eventually, Abe pried Jule's little fingers off the piano keys, and they started their all-night meeting. I went to bed. The next day there was a new battle plan. Scenes were to be shuffled and rewritten. Songs were going to be cut, new ones written. And this, while we played eight performances a week.

This is the fabled "On the Road High." Writers stay up all night, actors work and learn new things nonstop, often rehearsing a new scene in the afternoon, yet, at night, still having to play the old scene it's replacing. Subtle changes drive you crazy. It's hard to remember where you are. Often there has not been time for costumes and scenery to catch up with the material. So you could find yourself singing, "Good morning, Hawaii, how are you this sunny day" in front of a cunning igloo. That would be O.K. if you wanted a cheap sight gag (and who doesn't), but you get my point.

One night a scene change had to be covered and the new dialogue wasn't ready. They asked me if I would reprise a song I sang in the first act. I was thrilled—the more I had to do the better, even though I knew it was temporary. There was only one catch, they needed time to make the change. Sooo, my song, a spirited, lively, *fast* English-type madrigal, had to be sung very slowly and sadly and drawn-out. So there I was in my cheerful costume and bonnet singing ever so mournfully:

> *"I feel sorry for the girl*
> *Who hasn't got a beau*
> *Hasn't got a beau*
> *What a situation*
> *Specially in the springtime*
> *Fee-fi-fo-fum!"*

Not even the divine Sarah Bernhardt could have turned that sprightly aria into as bleak, black, and heart-rending a dirge as I did for a few days in Philadelphia. As long as they noisily changed the set beind me, I dragged out my song in front of a curtain. When all was quiet I brought it to a speedy end. When the new set was ready, I relinquished my second-act solo—and although it had become a company joke, I learned a great deal about the breaking down and acting of a song. I don't mean that I or anyone else in his or her right mind wants to distort or present a song in a style that's inappropriate, but learning the levels and possibilities of lyrics and imagining them in other situations is a real process for me. In my opinion, you ultimately discard your homework and sing the song simply and musically. It's rather like improvising before working on a scene.

Despite all the hard work and all the talented people involved, *First Impressions* did not do well on Broadway. I was singled out by Kenneth Tynan, among other critics, for my character authenticity. But I didn't get much of a chance to revel in the experience. The play closed quickly. If only Jane Austen had been available for rewrites.

FIVE

Preparing to play a Jane Austen character, I had read all her
books and many about her and her times. I had looked at draw-
ings and illustrations of what everything and everyone looked
like. The low-cut, high-bodiced long dresses and flat slippers
made me hold myself erect, and yet move with an easier fluidity.
My hair piled on top of my head, and a bonnet on top of that,
transformed my normal, everyday neck into a long and graceful
one. Contemporary manifestations of anxiety disappeared. My
hands would lie still in my lap, the left one palm up and gently
cupped, the right one in a relaxed fist that fit into it. No crossed
arms or sweaty palms on apricot silk. At moments of elation or
despair, my hands would go to the base of my throat, or possibly
one hand to my forehead or cheek. My musical numbers had to
be infused with the same delicacy and restraint. I had loved
becoming an inhabitant of Jane Austen's world. When the show
closed, I decided I wanted to go to England, to Europe, to the
Continent—alone.

I know this is no great big shakes now, or maybe it wasn't even
then. I knew almost no one there. It's true that Adolph was

I set out for my grand tour "filled with excitement, anticipation, very little fear, and very little money."

going to be in Paris, and that we made the vaguest, the vaguest nonplan to meet, maybe. You see, I wasn't even remotely sure how I felt about him. I wanted to have other romantic adventures on my first solo trip. I wanted to see what would happen, and yet the thought of meeting up with him in Paris where he had friends, a life, and where Sydney would be, too, was very appealing. Adolph had plans of his own as well. He surely liked me but he was going to go to Vevey, Switzerland, with Sydney and stay at Sydney's "old man's" and, also, he had another girlfriend who was going to be in Paris. The sly old puss.

So I go off to London filled with excitement, anticipation, very little fear, and very little money. I knew one person there, a darling English actor who had played my father in *First Impressions*. He had told me about an inexpensive hotel in Kensington. Now I need you to imagine what it felt like to go to a foreign country, when you didn't see it on TV every day and when it didn't cost a dollar ninety-eight to get there. The pre-drug high. "Oh, my God I can't believe it . . . me . . . me . . . I'm in actual London."

My English friend is happy to hear from me, and makes a date for lunch the *next* day. O.K. First day sight-seeing. Great. But what it's called is your first night in Europe alone. *Alone.*

I bought a ticket and went to see *A Taste of Honey.* It was theater, and English and wonderful. Then I took myself into some incredibly shitty—well, it would be the equivalent of a Times Square coffee shop near the theater and had a greasy something. I took a bus back to my hotel room which didn't seem so charming anymore, and pondered the sixty-four-shilling question. Was this girl from Jersey City really so independent, and so adventurous? I decided, yes, kept the lights on, and went to sleep. I spent the rest of my time in England looking, absorbing, but rarely spending time with people. I didn't much speak to anyone, or make friends—I was filling out some other section of my alternate life. I'm a Pisces, and more than half of my time is spent silently supplying conversation for myself and anyone else who's in my private scene.

"Would you like another one of these unfathomably thin perfect watercress sandwiches with your second delicately fragile porcelain cup of tea? Or should I just wipe the scone crumbs off your mouth with this discreetly monogrammed extra-weight damask napkin?

"Oh, yes, thank you so much, I'm quite pleased with my move from Jersey City to our flat in the Albany Mews right behind the palace. Yes, we're almost finished with the restoration of our cottage in Stratford that once belonged to Shakespeare's Uncle Lou.

"Do? . . . What do I do? . . . Oh, my dear Countess Maritza, . . . I manage to keep frightfully busy with my gardens, my dogs, my children, my Lord, and my voluminous, definitive book I'm writing on Middle English and how it grew!"

When I got to Paris, I went to my prearranged, travel-agent-recommended cheap hotel, and even I couldn't fantasize my way out of this one. It was a small, gray, dirty building on a street that was filled with similar buildings. The carpeting in the smoky, dingy lobby had a dirty orange and filthy tan pattern.

The peeling walls cheerlessly picked up one of those colors. There was a small concierge's desk behind which sat an old man whose coloring and look had taken on aspects of the rug. His eyes and ears were crusty. My French was fairly good; his was unintelligible. Four thousand years of Gallic charm and wit had escaped him. He allowed me to follow him up to my room. He allowed me to carry my own suitcases up the narrow stairs, through the barely lit gray halls. He opened the door, handed me a key, grunted something and closed the door. See Henny Youngman for "My hotel room was so small" jokes. Obviously the room had been decorated by the same imaginative sprite responsible for the lobby. The dreaded carpet, walls, bedspread, and curtains matched in some faded, filthy, ghoulish way, but at least it was well lit by the ubiquitous forty-watt naked light bulb in the middle of the very high ceiling. There was a gigantic armoire, so close to the bed that you couldn't open it to put your clothes away. A huge dusty armchair was stuck in one corner. I could imagine whiling away my time in it overlooking the bed. This wasn't working out.

I counted to *trois* and called Adolph. He was staying at the elegant Hotel Raphael. We had made no definite plans. I hadn't wanted to be hampered or restricted. Neither had he. Still, well, I mean, I didn't know one soul. He wasn't in. I left my name and number.

I didn't unpack, I took a walk and had lunch. I walked a long way to the Champs-Elysées and the famous Fouquet's Restaurant. I sat down on its terrace on the Champs, with my guidebook and my face held up to the sun. At the next table a Russian Auntie Mame–type lady and her husband were speaking English. Thank God she was effusive. She asked. I told. She lived in New York, too. They were staying at the Prince des Galles, a first-class hotel, right down the Avenue Georges Cinq. She gave me an aces travel tip. She told me that first-class hotels in Europe had top floors with small, clean, charming single rooms, without baths, which were originally for the maids of the wealthy. No one knew about them, you could always get one, and they were cheap. In her wonderfully funny, Old World, courtesan-like way, she explained that I would have a great address, lobby, service, and, as she explained, if you had half a brain, were young and pretty, you should do nothing but sleep there. Right? She told me to go back to my place and get my luggage. She would go and talk to her concierge and I could move in right away.

I did exactly as she told me. Back at the hotel I noticed with a vengeance that Adolph hadn't returned my call. I have always felt that death was preferable to showing anyone how needy or lonely you were. Still, well, I had to call him just once more to tell him my new location, and it *was* possible . . . This time he answered.

"Oh . . . I was just going to call you. I was so surprised to get your message . . . uh, when did you get here? Just uh, today. Have you been having fun?"

"Fun? Oh, Adolph, it's been thrilling. I'll tell you all about it when I see you. I'm moving to the Prince des Galles, maybe we could meet for . . . "

"Oh dear . . . oh . . . I feel awful, just awful . . . I can't . . . that is . . . I have to see some people . . . oh dear, if I had only known . . . Gee . . . I can't change . . . oh, Phyllis . . . tomorrow, we'll see Sydney. Gee . . . how . . . ?"

"Adolph, my God, don't be such a loon. You didn't even know I was coming; anyway I met these hilarious people at lunch, and they asked me to go to a party, but I just thought I'd check with you. Tomorrow? . . . Great. I'm just so excited to be here. I have to run, someone is picking me up to move me. Au revoir."

"Gee . . . it's great to hear your voice. I'll call you tomorrow. A party . . . that sounds like fun. Bye-bye."

Someone was picking me up to move me? Someone was picking me up to move me? Just a little Stella Dallas—that was me, a genius at quickly making up a life that didn't exist, or a liar. It depends on how kindly you feel at the moment. Never mind. I got myself to the spiffo hotel. The lobby and the help were gorgeous. The room was waiting as promised. A cell, a clean cell, but a good address. No TV, no radio, no view, but a good lobby. Of course, no one had asked me to anything. My Russian friends were not around. I didn't look for them, they had to think that, Adolph had to think that I . . . so my eyes filled with my ever popular tears. . . . I sniffed around the lobby, looking as if I were waiting for someone. I glanced at my watch a lot, the way Katharine Hepburn did in *Alice Adams*. I asked the concierge useless questions so that I could practice my French. And then I walked *up* the Champs-Elysées with the lights and the cafés filled with you-know-whats. I walked *down* the Champs-Elysées on the other side of the boulevard, airlines, touristy gift shops, the gorgeous Arc up ahead. I stopped at some café and had steak, frites, and a Coke. Sure, guys looked at me and tried to pick me up, but weirdo guys. That street, and those places at night, are not that funny, sweet, or harmless, but what the hell did I know? So I ate, walked some more, bought fashion magazines and chocolate, and went home to my Saint Francis of Assisi Memorial hotel room to fantasize the night I was having so I could tell Adolph and anyone else the next day.

"Yes, well, they took me to this party . . . oh, I'm not sure, somewhere on the Left Bank. A friend of theirs who had this gorgeous apartment overlooking the Seine and Notre Dame. I didn't know a soul, and they were all speaking French. I mean *pas un mot* of English . . . Well, I just gritted *mes dents* and got into a conversation with the nicest guy. He's a poet from a very rich and old French family . . . Jean-Pierre Bernard . . . he had a great sense of humor. First he laughed, nicely, of course, at some of my linguistic choices, but it was amazing, after a few minutes, it was as if I'd spoken French all my life. . . . Oh, to some sweet little café on the river. The food was to die and he was so nice. . . . Oh God! Nothing like that. We just had fun. He was impressed with where I was staying. I think he thought I was a closet millionairess. . . . No, I didn't tell him I was a closet closet. I didn't dare ask him up. Yes, it was a lovely way to spend my first night in Paris. . . . So, what's happening? . . . Sure, I'd love to come over and see how the rich live. . . . What time? What do you mean you got yourself into some things? I don't care, I really don't. I'll come along . . . no, I don't mind. I guess I thought you might be rather happy to see me . . . *remember me!* It's Phyllis, the dark one, the pretty one you were running after in the States. *Remember the States? Remember New York? Hello, is this Adolph? Ne quittez pas, I'm coming along for dinner. Now I remember why you drove me crazy. . . . "*

O.K., so we were both ambivalent. And I got sore as hell when I wasn't and he was, and he was only really sure he was serious about me when my ambivalence bordered on indifference.

I got to his hotel a little late so as not to appear remotely anxious. He had an elegant, old-money-looking suite. He was never a big spender, so I was surprised. The management had made a mistake, so they were giving it to him for the price of a room. We kissed hello, he hemmed and hawed, and looked so suspicious and darty-eyed and distracted that I wanted to sit on him to straighten him out. The house phone rang.

"Oh, yes . . . yes . . . yes . . . good . . . good . . . no . . . no . . . good . . . sure. . . . "

"That was Kathy," he said when he hung up. "She's on her way up. We're all going with Sydney, a whole gang . . . Moustache's . . . big table."

"That was WHO?"

I knew damn well who he had said, I just wanted to make him say her name again. Kathy! She was a supposed ex-girl of his. They had been a real thing. She was still nuts about him. She was living in Paris for a few months with her girlfriend. I hated her. She was old money, classy, Gentile, attractive, and smart, intellectual smart, not Jersey smart. She was a medium actress, but a well-done type for Adolph. Funny she wasn't, but she laughed at everything he said. She thought he was a genius. She didn't try to top him, or outshine him. She wasn't sarcastic. She was . . . oh, maybe . . . thirty. I was about twenty-four. I told Adolph, while Kathy was coming up in the elevator and as she was ringing the bell, that she was the type who would age badly and he'd better be careful. I was all heart.

She came in, she was too charming, and I was too livid. Poor lady, she was probably just as dismayed to find me there. God only knows what song-and-dance story Adolph *almost* told her. The three of us just had one enormous barrelful of laughs. Adolph was silent. She asked me polite questions about my trip. I made up adventures. They both looked dazed after about a half hour of my non-stop monologue.

O.K., kids, now what? We took a walk, we went into art galleries where she and Adolph exchanged knowing observations, while I prattled away about anything. I saw a print that I thought was terribly cute and Parisienne. It was ten bucks. I bought it. I could tell from the looks they gave each other and their faint "charming . . . are you sure you want it? Oh well, ten dollars . . . charming," that I had made some major artistic gaffe. I wasn't having a good time. We were supposed to meet at Moustache's in about an hour. I decided to let the two of them continue their saunter. I told them I'd meet them at the restaurant. They deserved each other . . . temporarily. I raced back to my cell, and did one of my usual take-out-every-piece-of-clothing, try-it-on, look-at-yourself numbers. I had to look great tonight. It wasn't easy to see myself. The only mirror was above a high chest of drawers. I had to stand on the bed to see anything. I put on a pink-and-white-checked gingham dress—V neck, sleeveless, tight-waisted. I was very tan, I looked good, fresh and saucy.

There was a long table, small candles glowing in little glass jars, bottles of red wine lined up looking so at home, and a Who's Who of Americans in Paris. I hugged and kissed Sydney. We were happy to see each other. He introduced me to novelist Irwin Shaw, a jolly, red-faced, raspy-voiced, curly-haired, interesting bear. I made as much stir as I knew how to in those days, before I went to sit at the place left for me next to Adolph. An adorable, tall, myopic, witty screenwriter named Harry Kurnitz was on my other side. "You know who" was sitting on Adolph's other side. She knew everybody there very well, so I assumed she was comfortable and in her element. I was once again, as I've so often told you, the new kid on the block. I was completely overstimulated by the place, the group, the atmosphere. At last I was going to have the kind of evening on this trip that I wanted. I felt hot, and funny, and pretty. The wine went right to my toes. I loved it that many of these older types responded to my humor and, I think, naturalness.

Sometime in the middle of this lively evening I felt Adolph grab my hand under the table. He left our two hands on my lap. He squeezed my hand, I squeezed his. I thought to myself, Yeah! . . . he is so proud of me. What a guy! What a girl! What a life!

Poor Kathy, poor kid, she's not really such a bad egg. I'll be nicer. And then for some reason, the tablecloth from our section of the table moved, and I looked down and saw that Adolph was holding Kathy's hand as well. This dreadnought, this poor excuse for a human person, had the nerve, the dopiness, to think that he somehow could . . . What? Placate? Hold on to? Not rock any boat in anybody's harbor? I yanked my hand away as if it had been burned. I felt like pulling the whole tablecloth and all its residents off in one magnificent, furious gesture. Adolph gave me his Hungarian, wounded-animal look. I gave him my Joan Crawford as Mildred Pierce look, and then turned sharply away. Remember those looks? Of course you do, they're still around and damned good.

I simply did not know what to do. I was much too angry and hurt. I didn't want to stalk out of there and screw up my evening, and yet I wanted to be taken seriously and I wanted him to like me better than her. I started laughing. I don't mean hysterically, but enough to make Harry, next to me, ask what was up. I whispered in his ear what had happened. He started laughing, too. I guess I instinctively realized that if it got to Sydney, he would turn it into an achingly funny routine, and then we'd all be off the hook. So I told him. He looked at Adolph. His eyes lit up and the rest of his face assumed a tsk! tsk! look. He waggled his finger at him: "Dolphus . . . you sneaky old fart." And then he started in on him. It was high low comedy. We were all screaming and crying with laughter, even Kathy. But I didn't know what it all meant to me, my trip, and my feeling that I could count on Adolph as a suitor, if I *needed* to.

I don't remember whom he dropped off first. I only know our plans were still vague, and he didn't say, "I'll never do that again." I linked up with other friends, I had some dates, but I really wanted to be with Adolph, and, I have to admit, the group —the smarts, the funnies, the action.

I started feeling very restless and slightly lost. One night after one of my other "dates," I went to join Adolph and Sydney at Moustache's again. It was late. There was no Kathy. Some of the gang had left. Adolph looked genuinely happy to see me. Sydney had had rather a few of his "marts" and was very expansive. Sydney said:

"Hey, Phyllis, how'd you like to come with the Dolphers and me to the old man's in the Switz? It's a lovely big mother of a dump . . . and the Oona is sweet, she's sweet, Phyllis. It's nice there, they're really rather sweet. . . . They've got all those little buggers running around, little shits, dividing my fucking inheritance even more. Every year the old Oona pops another one . . . and shit . . . a couple of mil less for Uncle Sydney. [He laughs. There is no real bitterness. Honest.] Come on, Phyllie, we'll have fun. They're really very sweet, it's up in the old Vevey. We'll have laughs. Old Pop goes to bed early, but Oona loves to stay up and gossip. We'll have laughs. . . . The kids are really sweet. Come on, Phyllie . . . you remember my old man! You know, the old turd with the derby and the cane . . . he's sweet, the old fucker. He's nice. Come on, Phyllie."

I couldn't resist that invitation and, God knows, why would I want to?

Color me *Jules and Jim*. Be reminded of Noel and Lynn and Alfred and Gertie. The three of us went off to Vevey, Switzerland, to visit Oona and Charlie Chaplin and family. The guys would stay at the house and I at a darling hotel on the lake in town. Not for propriety's sake, but for space sake.

You come upon the Chaplin house very suddenly. You drive on a winding road, turn a corner, and there it is on your right. You get no sense of it from that side, because its whole life is facing the other way, down green hills and valleys across the Alps. A covered porch, the width of the whole house, is where you have lunch, read, sit, talk, and look at a view that a great filmmaker would have chosen. The rooms are large and comfortable, like a relaxed English country house. Children, nannies, soft chairs, great food. The lady of the house is just that. Beautiful, intelligent, sharp, witty, soft-spoken, shy, a wonderfully responsive laugher who puts her hand over her mouth when she does.

"Oh, Charlie," when he compliments her.

"Oh, Charlie," when he does something funny. He doesn't often *say* anything funny, but he can pick up one of his small

Here we are with Oona and Charlie
Chaplin.

Adolph and Charlie.

children, hold her by her seat, and then look up with an expression that . . . oh, come on, we're talking Charlie Chaplin. You know what he does with a look, a gesture. When he chose to do it to illustrate something in a discussion of his films, it was the same. Except now he was a slightly stocky, round-stomached, white-haired man.

The Chaplins accepted me graciously. Aside from the obvious joy and awe I experienced being there, I also got to watch Adolph be as completely happy as I've ever seen him. I began realizing that my real competition was not going to be Kathy or Jujie or Lulie, but his idols, and his passion for work and the work of geniuses and artistic visionaries. He already had a real family of such people, including Betty, Lenny, Judy, and Sydney. They had their family jokes, events, history, language. I had to catch up, catch on, or be left out.

Do you know how it felt being there and watching and listening while Adolph hummed every note of Chaplin's movie scores, if called on, and filled in any word of a film title or bit of business? I looked at Adolph's face as Chaplin reminisced about the least known bit player, and realized that Adolph knew about it, had heard it twenty times, and was still completely captivated. Nothing else in the world mattered during those few days. He was like a poor kid who had been allowed into the rich people's house on the hill for Christmas . . . and this was Christmas. In many ways I loved him for these somewhat naive qualities. Yet I wanted to get on with my trip—to be experiencing things for the *first* time. I was tired of listening to other people's reminiscences, no matter how exalted. This must sound ungrateful, young. I was lucky to be there. And, yes, I know.

Here's a bit of extraneous information while we're in the comic-genius department. Groucho Marx was another of Adolph's idols and friends. Mine, too. His verbal humor was exactly as advertised. We got along great. He didn't reminisce as much as deflate. My kind of guy. I recently found a photograph of him dedicated to me. It says: "To Phyllis . . . not Adolph . . . not Betty . . . Love, Groucho."

Please don't worry. I'm not going to ask for your tears and donations for my problems with celebrities. Just bear with me as everyone's once said, and I'll get you and me out of this.

I left Switzerland alone, having had a good time, and went to Cannes to meet two pals and see that part of France. Once again I found the smallest room in the biggest hotel. My friends were young, funny, and not famous. Adolph joined us and fit right in. He also decided to accompany me to Rome, the next stop on my "itinerary." There, we were back on an "Adolph" schedule. Sitting around with "people" after dinner until very late, sleeping late, and not really seeing any of the sights.

One day in my Italian cell at the Excelsior Hotel, Adolph sort of asked me to marry him. Sort of, as only Adolph could. My response was a tiny tirade about how this was not the way I wanted to see Rome for the first time, sitting around talking about his past . . . etc. I went on and on.

He took my complaining seriously. Out we went while it was still light, to see the Colosseum. It was a crackly, clear sunny day. I'm walking around those powerful ruins, and trying to picture those times, those lions and togas, and crowds, but there is a buzz going on, a yammer that won't stop. It's Adolph.

"Phyllis, do you remember a great Smith and Dale vaudeville routine called Dr. Kronkeit?"

"No, I don't! And I don't care. I'm in Rome at the Colosseum, drinking in Rome, drinking in the Colosseum. Isn't this inspiring? Isn't this . . . "

"Oh, yes, inspiring, gorgeous." (He starts singing in a Jewish accent.) "Take off the coat, my friend" . . . (He's laughing.) "You see, a man comes into Dr. Kronkeit's office and the doctor sings, 'Take off the coat!' "

"Adolph, stop! O.K.? Please, I really don't want to hear a Smith and Dale routine, not while I'm at the Colosseum *for the first time*. Don't talk, Adolph. Don't sing. Just stop. Let me look, let me think. *Stop!*"

I'm saying this as deadly seriously as I know how, which is pretty good. I am becoming an expert on deadly serious with Adolph. I start walking much, much faster. Adolph starts walking much, much faster.

"Just listen to this. The doctor goes into an office, and the guy hears over the transom: '*Oh, you butcher!*' "

Adolph yells this the way Kronkeit must have yelled it. "You know whenever Lenny or Betty and I go to a dentist, or we're really upset we always . . . "

I am now running, and Adolph is keeping up with me and continuing his obsessive reminiscing. This goes on for a few minutes. I feel like I am losing my Italian marbles. I am so exasperated. And I am going crazy. I stop, out of breath. I grab Adolph and start shaking him. We are in the middle of the goddamned Colosseum.

"Stop it, Adolph! Stop it! Don't speak. Don't tell me another word. You are nuts. You are driving me crazy. *Go, leave, get out, leave me alone.* [I start crying.] Go away, don't apologize. Don't speak, just leave me alone. Now."

I am now crying uncontrollably. He is startled. I walk away. I can't see anything anymore. Why have I lost all of my sense of humor? Who's right? Who's wrong? Who cares? I'm knocked out.

A little later at the hotel, when I've calmed down, I tell him rationally that it's simply not working out between us, and he should leave. He calls Betty Bacall, who's in Biarritz, France. He goes. I'm fine about it. I'm back to being just a nice normal neurotic girl tourist. I finish out Rome, go on to Florence alone, and then to Venice. The gondolier who took me from the train station to my hotel asked me for a date. Why not? He was very attractive in his gondolier getup. When he came to pick me up that night . . . well, let's just say, something about the gondola gave him height and distinction. Adolph called. He'd like to come back and join me in Venice. He'll be good. He's been thinking. I'm right. Can he please? . . . Sure.

It *was* fine. He was charming and remorseful, trying to stop himself whenever he started a sentence with "During our first show . . ." or "Lenny and Betty and I always . . ." He tried to stick to the *now*, as they say now. I tried not to bristle at every *then*. He had to return to New York; I had a little bit left of my Grand Tour.

Ruth Dubonnet invited me to a friend's rented country house in Honfleur, an exquisite French fishing village on the Normandy coast. It was Jean-Louis Barrault's house (he wasn't in it), and everything was glorious, I didn't have to make it up. My fantasy came true. I felt that I had completed a real journey . . . a real experience. Still confused about Adolph, I went home.

A few weeks later, the friend I'd seen in the south of France and I went up to the Westport Playhouse in Connecticut, to see Adolph and Betty in their successful show called *A Party*. They were wonderful. I'd seen them perform before, of course, but something struck me about Adolph. It was like that little old devil Cupid in all those paintings. I suddenly fell hard . . . in real love, with real passion. My friend had a small sports car. The three of us drove home to New York. I sat on Adolph's lap all the way home, nuzzling him. He was surprised, so was my friend, so was I.

Adolph and I were now seeing each other with regularity. I began to feel more comfortable in his world. Some of his friends were becoming my friends as well.

I had always worked steadily, but I felt a new pressure to excel, not so much, though, that I changed my haphazard way of auditioning or choosing jobs. For example, the next play Abe Burrows directed was a good, solid, straight, nonmusical comedy. He offered me the ingenue lead. At the same time, I read for an English adaptation of a French play by Marcel Aymé called *Moonbirds*. The director was from one of the illustrious British rep theaters, and I was thrilled when he offered me a fairly small role in this completely bewildering play. I was weighing the two offers—it should have been no contest, right? I couldn't make up my mind. One was a career move, a step, on the path to building my visibility, but the other had Wally Cox,

My friends were young, funny, and not famous. Adolph fit right in.

Some of Adolph's friends were becoming my friends as well. *From left,* Betty Bacall, Leonard Bernstein, me, Shirley MacLaine, and Isaac Stern.

handsome Mark Rydell (who has become a top movie director) playing opposite me and putting his hand under my blouse on top of my bra'd bosom—in the late fifties that was hot stuff and embarrassing. Now it's just impossible and embarrassing. Then came the decisive piece of information. Harry Belafonte had come in as an associate producer. That did it. I visualized hanging out with Harry in Philadelphia, so I said yes.

I must tell you I never met or even laid eyes on Mr. Belafonte during the entire experience. I guess he was a silent producer, but I did get to go back to Philadelphia in yet another show that played to small but hostile audiences. The rewrites began, the producer took over directing after the sweet Englishman left after many huffs. Mark's hand and my bosom got very bored with that piece of business, which was mentioned by every critic. "Why?" was their unanimous reaction.

We came into New York and opened at the Cort Theatre. The opening went as you might expect—theatrically. Personally it was extremely nerve-racking and important. Adolph, who was by now a serious contender, was going to meet my parents for the first time.

It's intermission, and the small lobby of the Cort Theatre is filled with the usual cast of opening-night characters. Their conversation is loud, and they are looking around in an unfocused way. Everyone is smoking. The critics are out in the street or leaning against the walls. The backers of the show have a lot of family and friends with them. They are very dressed up, as if they were at an important family wedding. They ask *anyone* how they like the show. They seem very bewildered by *Moonbirds;* maybe they thought they'd get to hang out with Harry too. The Broadway wise guys are there, of course—they go to all the openings and make sure that everyone can see them sneering and looking superior. That's what they like to do. They go to Sardi's after the show and sneer some more over food. Then they stand and applaud and bravo when someone from the show walks in.

Finally, there are the families of the actors, stagehands, musicians, designers, and so forth, all of whom are enthusiastic and thrilled to be there. They are titillated by the "names." They can't stop stealing looks at them during the show.

I love my mother and father for always being enthusiastic and always thinking that I was "the best."

"Sig, I think that's him over there talking to Anne Jeffreys. He doesn't look *so* old. He's not *so* bad-looking. Is he, Sig? Is he *so* old or bad-looking?"

"Ray, he looks *my* age, he's skinny, and he looks like an Arab. He could be her father, for God's sake. I don't get it, Ray, I just don't get it. She could have anybody. What's the big deal?"

"Shah, Sig, he sees us, he's coming over. She told him to look for us. Oy, Sig."

"Mr. and Mrs. Newman? . . . Hello, I'm Adolph . . . well, isn't she wonderful?"

Playbill® is a registered trademark of Playbill, Incorporated, New York City. Used by permission.

Moonbirds opened on October 9, 1959. That same night, Adolph met my parents for the first time.

PHYLLIS NEWMAN
Sylvie

Following a Broadway début at the age six in *You'll See Stars*, Miss Newman w home to Jersey City to devote the n twelve years to scholarship. After atte ing grammar school, New Jersey's Linc School, Western Reserve and Colum Universities, she enrolled for acting cla with Wynn Handman in New York C to prepare for her adult theatrical car *Moonbirds* provides her fourth Broad assignment since her return to the st the others being *Wish You Were H Bells Are Ringing* as Judy Hollid standby, and *First Impressions* in wh she was featured as Jane. Miss Newma other appearances include an off-Bro way revue, *I Feel Wonderful*, the mo picture *Picnic*, and starring roles in vision's major dramas.

"Very pleased to meet you, I'm sure."

Daddy and Adolph shake hands. Momma smiles. Adolph talks about my qualities on the stage. Momma puffs up and out a bit.

"Yes, thank you, and she's such a good girl, such a good daughter. We're very proud of our little girl, aren't we, Sig?"

"Of course we are, why shouldn't we be, he knows that. Don't you know that, Mr. Green?"

"Adolph. She is . . . she is unspoiled . . . "

It goes on like that. It's time for the second act. The bosom bit is coming up. They go back to their seats.

"Sig, he's very nice . . . warm . . . I like him. Do you like him, Sig?"

"I like him, I like him . . . he's nice, but he's too old for my baby, Ray. He's been around, Ray, believe me, I know. I don't think I like it. He's been around, I know."

Don't ask me what that play was about. I didn't know then and I don't know now. It was fey. It was foreign. I waited in my flower-filled dressing room worrying. Was my acting all right? Was my bosom all right? What were my parents going to think about the scene? About Adolph? What was he going to think about them? Was this play going to run? Had I made a dreadful mistake in every department? Would this finish off my career, my family, my suitor? Is there a God? Am I blue? Well, you know the answers to all of the above. But here's how I found them out.

Adolph and my mother and father came backstage together. The experience of having sat dazedly through that play united them in some weird common bond. They all hugged and kissed me. They all phumphed . . . you know, uh, how do you say it . . . spoke elliptically. We went out to supper.

"So, do you think it was really necessary for him to put his hand, you know where? Does that make it modern or something?"

"I must say, I agree, Mrs. Newman, that was pretty gratuitous."

From then on we were home free, or at least home, marked down. Adolph was just his own odd self, but so warm. . . .

Skip the details, we decided to get married.

About a month before the wedding, I was at the Museum of Modern Art on a Sunday. I was alone. I spotted, among the crowd, a familiar hand holding a semifamiliar hand. No, not again, Yes. Yes, again. Sneaky Adolph was with, not Kathy, but a beautiful, well-born blonde, another supposed ex. Our six eyes couldn't believe it. I was polite. He was stricken. She was confused. He hadn't even told her we were about to . . . Oh well. That's it, folks. Enough's enough. True or false?

On the phone later, he had the dopiness to say that he only took her out this last time to tell her about us. I said something incredibly witty and appropriate like . . . "Stick it in your nose," a phrase that was seared into my brain from all my Jane Austen reading. Of course, he begged my forgiveness, my indulgence, my pity, and swore on some apocryphal Hungarian head that he would be faithful to me forever. I had a problem. I was in a dilemma. Three of my personal dwarfs—Angry, Uneasy, and Lonely—reappeared to engage me in endless internal chatter.

"All right just keep it down, guys, and listen up. . . . We've been through this before and we will again. Sure, I could call up 'the guy' and go another ten rounds with him, and sure there are plenty more where Adolph came from (God forbid!), but, you know what? . . . nobody is going to be *like* him . . . and guess what, guys, I even buy the faithful part."

I was right . . . and the only review I'm going to ask you to read is the one of our wedding.

BURT BOYAR'S NOTEBOOK
The Morning Telegram
February 3, 1960

Show business weddings follow the general tradition of all weddings. Someone plays "Here Comes the Bride," a man is shooting pictures for the wedding album, the bride and groom dance to their favorite song and most of the faces of the assembled guests are familiar. Well, that's sort of how it was at the Sunday night wedding of playwright Adolph Green and actress Phyllis Newman —but not quite. . . .

The ceremony took place in Adolph's apartment. Just as it was about to begin he realized he'd forgotten to hire a musician to play "Here Comes the Bride." Groom gets nervous and forgetful, y'know. However, all went well because by chance he had invited one. Composer Jule Styne sat down at the piano and played "Here Comes the Bride," and the wedding continued on schedule. "If I hadn't been there," said Jule, "Adolph would have had to play it himself."

THE RECEPTION was held at the Sheraton East, the former Ambassador Hotel. Here, too, things went according to traditional wedding procedure. There was a man walking around the room shooting pictures of the guests for a wedding album. The man in this case was Richard Avedon and the wedding album is to be his gift to the Greens.

The first dance was to a song called "Lucky to Be Me," from "On the Town," which put him and his collaborator, Betty Comden, on the map.

This is a good time to clarify the constant error people make in assuming that the team of Comden and Green are married to each other. They are not now and never have been man and wife, any more than Rodgers and Hammerstein are married to each other. Betty Comden is in private life Mrs. Steven Kyle.

THE FACES at this wedding were familiar . . . The bride and groom had their first dance together, then Abe Burrows cut in on Adolph and waltzed away with Phyllis . . . Ray Bolger spun

Adolph around the floor for a moment . . . That loosened it up a bit. The Leonard Bernsteins took the floor. They were dressed almost like twins, she in a black velvet suit and him in a distinguished looking black velvet dinner jacket. . . . George Abbott danced with Lauren Bacall. The 73-year-old Mr. Abbott is a tireless dancer. After watching him for a while someone said, "Gee. George is a great dancer!" "Yeah," was the negative reply, "but he's going to be sorry when he gets older."

Sydney Chaplin was with his fiancee, Noelle Adam . . . The Lawrence Langners, Farley Granger, Moss Hart and his wife, Kitty Carlisle, Martin Gabel and his wife Arlene Francis . . . Adolph's agent Irving Lazar who came in from Hollywood for the occasion . . . Phil Silvers and his wife Evelyn, Anita Loos . . . The Milton Greens, Ruth Dubonnet, Tom Guinzberg [sic] and Rita Gam.

MIDWAY through the dinner there was a tinkling of glasses. It was time for a toast. Sydney Chaplin stood and was about to speak, when from across the room Abe Burrows shouted angrily, "I was told there was to be no fund raising tonight!" That broke up the room. Finally, reasonable decorum was established again and Sydney said, "On behalf of Adolph, my dear, dear friend, and on behalf of Phyllis, my dear, dear—uh, friendess . . . " He spoke warmly about his friends and the guests drank a toast to the bride and groom. Adolph toasted his bride saying, "To my beautiful, unique and wonderful bride—this is the happiest night of my life."

The dancing resumed. Lester Lanin's music was sensational . . . The Henry Fondas stopped in for a drink . . . Arlene Francis left to do her "What's My Line?" guessing and returned right after it . . . Mike Nichols stopped by . . . Arthur Laurents Charleston'd with Richard Rodgers' daughter, Mary.

IT WAS a wonderful party . . . Excellent wines, delicious food and wonderful people . . . I guess I will always be a small boy about certain things like turning around and finding that the man I just bumped into on the dance floor was Ray Bolger. . . .

I watched Lester Lanin wave his arms and conducting like mad and I wondered how he felt as Bernstein, the conductor of the N.Y. Philharmonic, danced by.

This is the first time I've ever reviewed a wedding. It was a smash. The best damn marriage of the year. I hope it runs forever!

SIX

Adolph and I both wanted children whenever they would arrive. Three months after we were married, I found myself pregnant. I had just gotten a job on a television series called "Diagnosis: Unknown." It starred Patrick O'Neal as a brilliant, crime-solving pathologist. I played his adoring, wisecracking assistant. By the time the second or third show was being taped, I started getting blimplike, and also very sleepy. I remember little about the show because I dozed on the set whenever I wasn't needed, which given my looks at the moment, was a lot of the time. My part got smaller and smaller . . . my lab coat got bigger and bigger . . . and the camera had to come in closer and closer. I roused myself to arch my eyebrow every so often and called it a day.

After one of the shows, Patrick invited Adolph and me home to a small gathering. At that time, he and his wife lived in a couple of floors of a brownstone in the Village. We got there, walked up the flight of stone steps outside and, like the timing of a good joke, the door was opened swiftly, energetically, before we expected it.

95

Patrick O'Neal and me in *Diagnosis Unknown*.

"HI! . . . I'm Cynthia!"

And she certainly was.

Cynthia Baxter O'Neal. It would take Fitzgerald and Tolstoy working as a team to do justice to her many-layered life and times. Her impact is strong and immediate, initially because of her startling and individual physical beauty, and then . . . rat-a-tat, you "get" her unforced charm, unfrenetic vitality, and intellect and instinct, infectious enthusiasm . . . and finally a touch of naughtiness.

Cynthia was a very young, talented, working actress when she met and married Patrick. She's uncomfortable being the object of public attention, so it was no hardship for her to stop. Through the years she has been offered many acting jobs, but the only time she accepted was when her friend Mike Nichols asked her to do a scene with Jack Nicholson and Art Garfunkel in the movie *Carnal Knowledge*. "Hard to resist that one," she said.

In one of the many previous lives that she's sure she's had, she was probably the cutest, most popular guru on the block. It is impossible to resist getting involved with her constantly growing interests and enthusiasms.

"Phyllis, my flower, my hyacinth, my buttercup, I'm nuts about this analyst. He's simply amazing. He got my number in one second. He won't let me get away with any of my tricks. We spent the first few minutes talking about the latest episode of 'Upstairs, Downstairs.' We scream with laughter, he's one of us . . . not at all stuffy. You know, you really ought to see him. You'd like him. And he would make you feel better (pause); he can see you tomorrow at three-fifteen; I made an appointment for you."

It didn't work out; he looked at his watch constantly, and I wanted to kill him. I stopped going after three or four visits. Cynthia grew disenchanted with him as well. After the last episode of "Upstairs, Downstairs," there didn't seem to be all that much to talk about.

"Oh, Phyllis, I am just . . . blown away. I have never experienced anything like this weekend. A lot of it was painful, but I've broken through feelings, and had insights that no asshole analyst—not Freud himself—could ever accomplish. There was so much love in that room. It was a completely comfortable and protected space. You must have this experience."

"I don't think so."

"I just don't understand why you're resisting this."

"Oh, Cynth, the thought of 'sharing' in front of a few hundred people is my idea of hell. I'm sure it works for you, for others . . . but I'm just . . . too fine, I guess."

She has never become angry or apparently aggressive, just bemused, wondering why I couldn't accept and share these enlightening experiences she had discovered.

A biggie was est. The only way I thought I could weasel out was by agreeing to do it only if Werner Erhard (its charismatic founder) would supervise my training personally. I felt completely safe, because at that time he was an enormous attraction and was always traveling and lecturing to gigantic audiences at places like Radio City Music Hall. He no longer did the smaller training sessions.

"Hello, my sweet, my Jujube, my Nestlé's Crunch . . . you'd best clear the next two weekends . . . guess who's coming to get you to 'get it'? "

So I spent four twenty-hour days along with five or six hundred other people, on hard chairs, in a hotel ballroom opposite Penn Station. It was like an abusive revival meeting. Erhard was impressive and dynamic. His program was brilliantly conceived. It encompassed many different disciplines and used some relaxation techniques that I remembered from my father's days as a hypnotist, but it was an original adventure. Aspects of it were useful and intriguing and for a while I was convinced that "I'm O.K., you're O.K."—but *they're* shits.

I've followed Cynthia through vegetarianism, the Pritikin Diet, Food Combining, Louise Hay's remarkable healing pro-

Cynthia O'Neal, Steve Sondheim, and me at Cynthia and Patrick's twenty-fifth-anniversary party.

cess, nutritionists, chiropractic adjustments, and anonymous meetings. We shared a SoHo loft where she designed and I wrote and we both pretended to be single. We wended our way through avant garde dance companies, permed our hair, and exchanged epic phone calls. Most of those calls begin normally but move quickly on to antic and fanciful improvisations. We push each other into an exclusive world of the absurd. If, instead of spending all that money with the phone company, we had invested it in, say, real estate, by now she and I would own Montana.

She has stood by me through the dark times, and she's always been there to share the joy.

She was with me for the birth of both my children. Adam was born on January 11, 1961. Five minutes after I got back to my hospital room Cynthia burst through the door. "We've got to fill out college applications . . . never too early, gumdrop."

And, when Amanda arrived on December 29, 1964, she was there: "Well, you've done it, lamb chop—you've produced a beauty—she looks exactly like Auntie Cynthia."

You can call me a sentimental fool, but those days when my children were born were the two happiest and most comfortable days I've ever had. Those were the moments that set the standards by which most other moments fail. It was how it was meant to be, for me, in the cosmic sense. My feelings were pure. I wanted to be these children's mother. I don't mean to suggest that I have been, or am, an unselfish or even a good mother. (I would if I thought my kids would let me get away with it.) But it's my natural state, and not even the most difficult times have shaken that belief.

After Adam's birth, Adolph, Betty, and Jule Styne were working on a musical based on a book of short stories by Edmund G. Love, *Subways Are for Sleeping*. The characters and situations were based on real fringe people whom Mr. Love had run into during some bleak years of his. One of the characters was Martha Vail, an attractive blond beauty-contest loser from the South. When she could no longer pay her rent for her seedy apartment, the landlord threw her out with all her suitcases of clothes. She snuck back in, and, dressed only in a towel, stayed for a long time. Whenever the landlord came to the door she would threaten to drop the towel and scream. I thought it would be a terrific part.

Adolph and I had never discussed working together up to that point. It wasn't an issue. I didn't expect him to make me a star, nor did I ever, ever ask for help from him or his friends. I was a busy, professional actress and singer.

Both Adolph and Betty thought that I would be very good in the part. Jule, of course, had hired me for a less likely role in *First Impressions* and to this day is my biggest supporter. I didn't know the director, Michael Kidd. The producer, the then omnipotentate of Broadway, David Merrick, didn't know my work, plus, on principle—his own made up for this occasion only—he objected to the wife of one of the authors being cast. They agreed to audition me, along with every other singer/actress in New York between the ages of twelve and ninety-three. I prepared for that audition with more care than I ever had before. I was in good voice, I had worked on the scene. The Southern accent came effortlessly to me. I was looking and feeling good until I walked into that theater and saw all the other young women looking and feeling equally good. A lot of them were people I had worked with or knew through classes. They looked at me with incredulity and pure hatred. What the hell was I doing auditioning for my own husband's show? Was it just for appearance' sake . . . so that no one could yell nepotism, or foul if they didn't know that word? Or was my husband just humoring me? Did he think I was an untalented clod? Did I have the part already? Who did I think I was or wasn't? I had to wait a long time. No preferential treatment.

I've already told you of my normal garden-variety audition neuroses. This was becoming worthy of a textbook. When I finally got onto the stage I felt like a frozen potato. As usual, I made jokes as I tried to make my arms and legs move at the joints.

"Hi . . . hi . . . hi . . . Hihihi . . . hi!"

Michael Kidd tried to ease the situation. He told me how much he was looking forward to hearing me. He asked me: "Which would you rather do first? Read or sing?"

"Ring! . . . I mean sead!" I responded button quick and hopelessly muddled.

They all laughed quarter-heartedly at my insane nervousness, while Adolph was probably vomiting into the blackened seat beside him.

You know, God takes care of good-hearted fools. I sang and read really well. No one could deny that. I became that charming Southern loser as I read the scene, and somehow that famed adrenaline went right where it belonged—to my vocal cords. I knew I had done well, I hadn't disgraced my husband. The compliments from everyone but Mr. Merrick were sincere.

Adolph told me that night how proud he was of me, and yes they thought I was terrific, but . . . he didn't think I had a good chance. There was a lot of resistance. He wouldn't tell me who or why. I've told you he's often evasive, not exactly forthcoming when complicated and uncomfortable situations arise involving me and his one life and Betty and other colleagues in his other, work life. It's completely understandable and completely infuriating and frustrating. In those days I never pressed. My misguided code of ethics and honor (and fantasy) was, don't show you're needy, don't be intrusive or interfering, don't let your ambition or talent be taken too seriously—his is the career that's big stuff—laugh it off, be well adjusted. Wrong, a thousand times, wrong. If I had my life to live over, and I might, I would realize that it isn't "unfeminine" or "pushy" to use all the resources available to you to fulfill your own creative life as well as your significant other's. Somehow, I felt I would be betraying him if I became too successful.

There was nothing I could do but wait to hear from the casting office. I knew through my agent that they had cast other principal parts with Carol Lawrence, Orson Bean, and Sydney Chaplin. And I knew also that not since the search for Scarlett had there been so many women scrutinized for this comparatively minor role. They asked me to audition again. I did. I waited backstage one more time, hearing "my scene" being read over and over. My turn came.

"Hi . . . hi . . . hi . . . should I sing the same song I sang the last forty times? You know this is the first time I ever heard of *NOT sleeping with the author to get the part* . . . I know, I know, just shut up and sing."

I *still* did not get the part. Rehearsals were drawing closer, and by now I think everybody would have been happier if they never had to see me again. They couldn't find anyone they liked better. Adolph completely absented himself from discussing others' merits versus mine. It was awful for him . . . and for me. I have sat in on casting discussions and they are pretty "blunt."

"That broad will never see thirty again. She's got fat legs and no tits. Her voice is so-so. Every man in the audience should want to lay her, not cover his eyes with the program."

That *of course* was a made-up composite sentence to illustrate my point. And that was a long time ago. Now, of course, what with our raised collective consciousnesses, our people-free closets, Ted Koppel and "Nightline," the critiques are much gentler and nondiscriminatory.

"It seems to me that this woman, though very musical and charming, isn't 'fit' enough, that is to say, her body is not contemporary, and therefore she doesn't give off a sensual enough aura . . . if you see what I mean? But what do you think?"

Theater casting has come a long way, but we have miles to go before we sleep.

I had really given up on it when my agent called and said, "You won't believe this. They want you to come in and audition again, in a blond wig and a towel."

"This is ridiculous, I won't do it. They just want to humiliate me again, but this time with no clothes on. Tell them no, no!"

"You're making a mistake. . . . I'm telling you, they really can't find anyone who impressed them like you did. Hang in, Phyllis; if this goes well, they'll have to give it to you."

I rented a blond wig, and spent hours in front of the mirror trying to drape a towel around me that would stay in place while I sang and moved about.

Sorry, but you have to know that I'm thinking of what it feels like now to wrap a towel around this funny old body, and how baths and showers used to be luxurious and therapeutic and now they are to be gotten over with quickly. Unfortunately, for many women, they are the time to check for uninvited changes, and they're so relieved when another bath goes by trouble free.

I felt ashamed and angry while I was changing into my garb at the theater. It's harder to keep your fake dignity when you're almost naked and in high heels and a wig. Somehow I did it. This time there was applause when I walked out. I knew that I was going to get the part, and I thought my troubles were over.

Rehearsals went well, my scenes were all with Orson. I wasn't around much for the rest of the time. We read only the first act on the first day, so it was apparent that there was still work to be done. It was a difficult task to combine the disparate stories and construct a plot which would involve the audience with the hero and heroine. Orson and I were playing eccentrics with built-in character conflicts. Our scenes together were funny and the most realized, I thought.

I had one song in the first act. It was a long, funny piece called "I Was a Shoo In," in which Martha tells her tragic tale and illustrates what she did for the talent section of the beauty contest. Betty and Adolph are probably the best and wittiest writers of character material for the musical comedy theater. I say this with complete prejudice but also insider knowledge of the way they and Leonard Bernstein, for example, were able to take both the brilliance of Rosalind Russell as a comedienne and her limitations as a singer and write a song that was perfect for the character of Ruth in *Wonderful Town*. She told them she could sing four notes only and that she needed a song that would go: Da . . . da . . . da . . . da . . . da . . . da . . . da . . . da . . . joke. Out of that conversation came the song "One Hundred Easy Ways to Lose a Man."

Then, of course, for their great friend Judy Holliday in *Bells Are Ringing* they created the telephone-answering operator who lives through her customers' lives. With Jule Styne, they wrote a scoreful of songs that became popular like "Just in Time" and "The Party's Over," but also "I'm Going Back Where I Can Be Me to the Bonjour Tristesse Brassière Company," "Drop That Name," and many more. Again they incorporated the character's needs with the strengths, idiosyncrasies, and personality of Judy. For *Peter Pan,* they knew that Mary Martin had a beautiful coloratura part of her voice as well as the rich middle section, so they wrote "Mysterious Lady" which used them both. Since they are such good performers themselves, their connection with the needs of other performers is immediate.

In my case they fashioned a number to my skills and strengths. It was a performer's or rather, this performer's, dream.

About two weeks after rehearsals started we had a very rough run-through for the director, authors and producer. I'm very slow in rehearsals—not in learning lines or songs, but in finding the character, the humor, and energy. I studied acting for many years with the inspired Wynn Handman.

One aspect of the "method" I learned in Wynn's classes is to build slowly, filling in little details as I go along. That often worries the people who've hired me. I look distracted, I don't seem energetic in the right way, I'm nervous, and seem unsure until it comes together. I pay little attention to my appearance during rehearsals. I've been told by many directors, including Bob Fosse and Mike Nichols, how concerned they were about me at some point during rehearsals. . . . Well, you've got it. During *Subways,* I was all of the above and dressed in ill-fitting rehearsal clothes and no makeup for the run-through, and some of the creative team panicked. David Merrick decided that the audience would never buy me as a beauty-contest aspirant, that I wasn't sexy. He totally forgot how I looked at the audition. He insisted that a great deal of my part be cut. It killed Adolph. He knew. But he was in that famous untenable position. The next day he and Betty were in the very next room from me in my very own apartment, cutting my part way down.

Rehearsals, previews, everything from then on was shaky and depressing for me. I was afraid I would be fired, I was afraid Adolph had a flop on his hands; it was as if my varied emotions were thrown into a blender every day. I wanted the play to succeed. But with me. I honestly felt that I had a lot to contribute. Adolph was my husband, my friend. But he would have to go along with the "other side." He had no singular power. He had all those fears *and* the show was not working. Carol and Sydney were anarchistic; they hated their parts and would go off and try to rewrite them.

We finally got to Philadelphia, the first tryout town. Adolph and I, Baby Adam and a young nanny, were in a big suite at a hotel. The contrast of our happy baby and the joy of his little protected world with the agonies, duplicity, and despair we each had at the theater was startling.

Merrick was really on my case. He discussed endless variations on my theme over and over again with Adolph and Betty. He was obviously getting some kind of thrill from torturing them. On the opening night in Philadelphia, the first couple of scenes played all right. It was my cue . . . my mouth felt lined with cotton, my wig hurt, I was afraid that my towel would slip and was sure that this would be my first and last performance in *Subways*.

The lights hit me, and as soon as the audience saw me and my towel I got applause and a laugh, and since home to me is any stage where I'm doing well, I got out of the way and let Martha tell her story and do her act. Both Orson and I were getting terrific audience response throughout our scene, and when I finished the song "Shoo In" ("They may have gotten a surrender from Robert E. Lee but never . . . never . . . never . . . never . . . never . . . from me . . . *never!*"), there was that sound, that crack, that rush—solid and spontaneous applause, cheers. We couldn't continue with the scene. I just stood there grinning at Orson and he at me. It was a genuine made-in-America ovation, an honest "She stopped the show."

Betty and Adolph were standing in the back of the orchestra, behind the audience. Betty burst into tears. They hugged each other. The always surprising Mr. Merrick said to Adolph at intermission: "Well . . . how do we make the whole show about her? Then we'd have a hit."

Phyllis Newman and Orson Bean in "Subways"

Subways' Phyllis Newman
Is Toweled Show-Stopper

The show got bad reviews. I got those once-in-a-lifetime discovery raves and attention. No, I'm certainly not going to quote them in my very own book, unless you twist my arm or send me a self-addressed stamped envelope and a dollar to cover the cost of my apartment maintenance.

It was heady stuff for me and back to work for everyone else. Over one weekend, Betty and Adolph rewrote the entire female lead character, new songs were put in, things got better. We moved to Boston. Same response. A little bit of what was cut from my part was restored, but not much. Feelings were too strained. The leading characters still needed work.

No matter how experienced you are, and how many shows you've written, directed, produced, or acted in, there comes the moment when all objectivity is lost, and slight advances, or fixes, or a better audience response deludes you into thinking that the problems have been solved. Nothing creative would ever be finished if we were a mass of cool, analytical, detached workers, rather than people who operate on emotional drive, people whose need to communicate using their given talent surpasses most practical considerations. I have to believe I'm Martha Vail trying to stay alive. I have to be vocalized, exercised, secure in the character before I step out on the stage. The minute I stand aside from her and become Phyllis Newman, worrying about the note I sang, or comparing tonight's laughs with last night's, something goes out of the performance. I can't be embarrassed by the material, or too self-involved with my newly won acceptance. I can't call attention to myself; the attention must come from the audience's interest in *her*. That's the crucial difference, in my opinion, between an actress and an entertainer. I've tried to be both. On a nightclub floor, or a television variety show, being myself has been comfortable and appropriate.

No miracle occurred opening night in New York. The reviews were mixed to poor. David Merrick took out a full-page ad for the show in *The New York Times* with rave quotes from all the leading critics. The abominable showman had found men with the same names as those critics and got them to give quotes. It was a truly original stunt. Everyone talked about it. *The Times*, of course, stopped running the ad as soon as it realized it was a fake, but the publicity probably helped the show to run the six months it did.

David Merrick had another show that season—*I Can Get It for You Wholesale*—which introduced Barbra Streisand, and when the Tony nominations were announced, I was amazed and delighted to have been nominated along with Barbra Streisand, Barbara Harris, and Elizabeth Allen. That was before the Tony Awards were televised from a theater. Then, the ceremony took place in a hotel ballroom and we all sat at tables and had dinner. I was sitting next to David Merrick, who was still not too crazy about me. As they read the nominees' names in my category, he turned to me and said, "I voted for Barbra . . . she's going to

This was taken the night I won the Tony. With Adolph and me are Betty Comden Kyle and her husband, Steven Kyle.

win." I was too stunned to respond, I didn't have time. I heard my name being announced as the winner. I let out the special winner's shriek, looked at Mr. Merrick for that split second you dream about in just deserts heaven, and ran up to the microphone to get my award before the committee and the gods changed their minds.

Sweet satisfaction. I beamed, he glowered. When I got to the mike a strange small figure was up there with me. His name was Stan Berman and he was a notorious gate-crasher around town at the time. I was furious. I nudged him aside, the way Marilyn Cooper had nudged me aside some twenty years earlier, and said, "You're not going to rob me of my big moment." He didn't . . . nobody could.

SEVEN

After *Subways*, the theatrical world was my oyster, my clam, and my cheeseburger medium rare. I can't begin to tell you what I was offered on Broadway and on California-based sitcom television. If I could, I would embellish it as only an actress speaking of rejected parts or a businessman speaking of missed real-estate deals can. Why did I turn them down? Because I loved my life, my "man," my baby boy, my apartment, my second pregnancy, and then my new baby girl.

During those early sixties years, "YOU CAN HAVE IT ALL" were not among the five most frequently used words by grown women. I, frankly, didn't know how to be as absorbed as was necessary to plot, plan, and work at a major career, and maintain the pleasure I got from my personal life.

Instead I got very active on television game shows, especially the very best of them which were produced by Goodson-Todman in New York. I had a good time and got paid for doing what I normally did for nothing in people's living rooms. They didn't take a great deal of time. We would tape five shows in one

Adam.   Amanda.

day. They required little rehearsal or preparation except for major teasing of the hair.

Leland Hayward was then producing a live satirical television show called "That Was the Week That Was." I auditioned by singing my interpretation of Streisand's interpretation of "Happy Days Are Here Again." They hired me to sing it on the next week's show and I stayed for two seasons. It was a precursor of "Saturday Night Live" and a stimulating show to be with. It had been a great success in England hosted by David Frost and he brought it to the United States. Herb Sargent, Buck Henry, and Gloria Steinem were among the writers, but they were frustrated by the censorial ways of network programming. Often, whole pieces would be cut or changed between the dress rehearsal and the show. Many weeks the writers would choose a well-known woman for me to satirize. I sucked in my cheeks and my chest for Audrey Hepburn, planted my hand on my hips and thrust out my chest for Sophia Loren, deadened my eyes for Lynda Bird Johnson, and slurred my speech for Judy Garland. I found that I was "born to mimic," to characterize—really

After *Subways,* my life
revolved around Adam,
Amanda, and Adolph.

not to reproduce the sound or the look of someone, but to search out what it felt like to be that person—and try to inhabit her body using her broad character traits as a guideline; it was working from the outside to get inside to be able to exaggerate, in a comic way, the outside, as Stanislavski never said.

Around that time I was booked to appear on one of the first "Tonight" shows to be hosted by Johnny Carson, which originated in New York as well. Johnny was like the guy I would have picked out to talk to in a room full of equal winners—attractive, smart, fresh, and funny. I made dozens of appearances and was the first woman to host the show when he was away.

He made me laugh, not in a pushed show business way, but honestly and heartily. . . . People still stop and ask me to "laugh for us." I try to explain nicely that I can't do it on command, as I chuckle halfheartedly so they won't go away mad or think I'm an ungrateful wretch.

Some people's lives are cabarets, old chums, but mine seems to be an incessant war . . . with myself. How can I complain about those years? Watch. As years went on, although I was doing other professional things, I certainly was best known for the Carson show. I rarely went on there to sell anything, except myself, and I was beginning to dislike the product.

They prepare you for the show by having one of their very smart and experienced talent coordinators call you to discuss what you will be talking about. They try to construct a general outline or plan so that both the guest and Johnny have places to go if they get stuck, or the conversation falters. I would try to think of interesting or provocative subjects, and although I was very active politically through those years and had strong opinions on any number of social issues, I realized that they would have sounded foolish and frivolous coming out of the character I found myself playing. By exaggerating some of my personal qualities, and not having anyone else to satirize, I seemed to be unconsciously parodying myself. I was worried that I would turn into that "quintessential talk show guest" we all knew—the one who finishes her double-time arrangement (with added conga drums) of "I've Got to Be Me," bows ever so deeply to the scattering of applause, blows kisses to the audience, and slightly out of breath says:

"Thank you—thank you—thank you—super—super—let's hear it for Doc and the band . . . thanks, guys . . . Oh, Johnny, I love that song—such fun—such soul—such truth—such lyrics. Oh, I feel great . . . I always feel great out here in California. Oh, by the way I open in Tahoe on the twelfth, Vegas on the thirteenth, Reno on the fourteenth . . . and close on the eleventh. . . . Thank you. Oh, and I forgot that my book, *Laughing Your Way from the Kitchen to Death,* will hit your bookstores on the fifteenth—and I'll be around to autograph copies, in New Jersey on the nineteenth, New York on thc twentieth, New Mexico on the twenty-first, New London, New Hampshire and New Haven on the twenty-second and New Guinea in March.

One of my appearances on "The Tonight Show" with Johnny Carson and Ed McMahon and my fellow guests, Sammy Davis, Jr., and Burt Reynolds.

"Seriously though, ladies and gentlemen, we tend to view this whole talk show scene a little too lightly for my money. We are all here just for you . . . the little people at home. . . . Say! . . . How many of you out there are really sick? Let's see hands . . . O.K. How many of you are post- or non-coital? . . . O.K. Good. . . . How many dead asleep? . . . Let's hear snores . . . terrific . . . And . . . how many of you are just plain dead? . . . Sensational. . . . We're here to live, talk, plug, and get rich for you and you and you. . . . We Are Your Life."

Of course, I exaggerate. The truth is that I rarely remembered the "points" to be hit. I honestly tried to engage Johnny in conversation and we had spontaneous fun. But, after my segment was finished and I had moved out of the Main Chair to make way for the next guest, I started obsessing over whether I had made a fool of myself. God knows, I have plenty of times in my life . . . when I talked too much or too little, came on too strong or too weak, bared my soul when no one cared, used the wrong tense, touched a hand only to have it stiffen, or mistook a kindly look for lust.

The school that Adam was going to at that time had "Class Teas" which the mommies had better attend. I wasn't thrilled but I threw on a black turtleneck sweater, skirt, boots, and gold chains. That was the official New York with-it Mother uniform. I put on extra-heavy eyeliner so that I wouldn't look *too* sedate, and a long expensive fur coat to drive home the success bit. It seemed sacrilegious to stuff my coat next to all those sensible gray cloth coats or bizarre "fun furs," on the wobbly pipelike hanging rack. So I kept it on my shoulders as Michael Curtiz had when he'd visited backstage at *I Feel Wonderful.*

I had seen the other mothers only occasionally at other school functions. I knew one or two of them well enough to say hello and "Well . . . how's Claude or Joshua doing this year?" End of conversation for me. I tuned out while the mother droned on about lack of initiative or overachieving or underwhelming. I was always the only mother who would spend at least twenty-five of the allotted thirty minutes of the "Tea" part eating. The class mothers made about two hundred tea sandwiches. There was watercress on white bread, pimiento and cream cheese on white bread, and an occasional maverick of tuna on only slightly less than white bread. The other mothers would eat one or two discreetly, but I appeared to have eaten last sometime during the Korean conflict. I pushed those dry cottonlike squares into my mouth, one after the other, barely taking the time to swallow.

It was funny how the mothers, for the most part, avoided me. After all I was a semicelebrity. They chatted so easily, they shared ski trips, pediatricians, leagues of women somethings. No one was interested in last week's *Variety* grosses, or the word on the preview of the new Barbra Streisand film.

After the sandwiches, we went into Adam's fifth-grade classroom and sat at the obscenely undersized desks that made it look like a scene from *Alice in Wonderland*. We listened as the new headmaster got off a few then "now" remarks about the quality of life in the ghetto which bordered the school, and how with our help ... blah ... blah ... Then he introduced Adam's teacher, Mr. Towns, about whom I'd not heard much.

He was a knockout, a tall, aesthetic, athletic looker in bottle-green corduroy and long hair. He explained, in a slightly affected manner but with real enthusiasm, what he was trying to accomplish, his views on education and his real love for teaching and reading and poetry and liberal politics and ... he was really cute. I was sorry that I hadn't gone with my natural young-bohemian look ... which he would have liked. His jokes weren't bad, not boffo but sweet. He was nice, very nice. After he finished his explanation of the classwork, he asked for questions. He urged us not to make them personal about our specific children, but rather of general interest. I tried desperately to think of a question. Since I hadn't been listening, but fantasizing erotically ... I couldn't. When it looked as though we were about to break up without my getting a shot at anything, I raised my hand and asked, "What do you do about sex?" It got a mild laugh. On the Carson show it would have been worth at least double that. "What I meant to say was ... don't you find that boys of this age are preoccupied with it and do you have good healthy discussions?" I slumped to my seat in what could charitably be described as awkward silence. . . . But God bless Mister Wonderful, he started talking immediately, and turned my impulsive question into a passable exchange. I waited until almost everyone had left to inspect the new library and made my halting apology. "I really shouldn't be let out with normal people. I'm sorry. And please don't take it out on Adam. He's a terrific kid. He really is crazy about you, and I liked what you said so much."

"Listen," he said, "I'm an enormous admirer of yours. Whenever you're on the Carson show, we stay up and watch. You're really funny and you have a unique take on everything. Don't worry about these other mothers; they're very nice, but they must have mixed feelings of admiration and jealousy toward you, because you've done so much more with your life than they have, and you are, after all, a pretty glamorous creature." He then gave me a noncrooked, dazzling young smile . . . and, gentlemen of the jury, I rest my case.

During the next few days, between singing lessons, lying in bed, dinner parties, and trying to listen to what my children were saying, I gave a lot of thought to some hugely imaginative conceivable situations with Mr. Towns. He was roughly twenty-five or twenty-six, and I was roughly thirty or forty. He was roughly a newlywed and I was roughly not really unhappily married. In fact on a scale of one to ten, I would give it a comfortable seven, maybe even eight, whereas my friends were lucky if they were three or fouring it. But let's face it. What the hell would he want with me, who needs the aggravation and how could I pull it off?

I sounded out friends who I suspected had led a more colorful extramarital twilight life than I. That would be almost anybody. I got some particularly good advice from the vegetable clerk at Gristede's: "Don't bug me, lady, I got my own problems." And so it went, the days getting draggier and the nights more and more filled with adolescent imaginings.

My big break came in the form of a lousy report card. "C−, C, sloppy work—doesn't pay attention, in danger of failing, etc." Well, I can tell you it gladdened this mother's heart. And when my husband and son came in later that day, I went into my "Who the hell does he think he is, giving my little genius that rotten report card?" bit.

My son went along with it, of course, explaining how some kid on the bus had stolen all his homework all month. My husband took the teacher's side and I allowed myself to be persuaded to phone Mr. Towns and have a serious discussion about Adam's work, and work habits. He explained that he'd expected to hear from us and that he had undermarked him for a reason. Before he could go on, I said, "I'm sorry, but I find it very difficult to discuss this on the phone, as I have a phone phobia and can't speak more than three minutes, so could I meet you after school in front of the school building and we can take tea together and speak—good-bye." After I hung up I wondered where all that had come from. Maybe from Louise, the goddess of infidelity who watches over slightly hysterical married ladies.

By eleven-thirty the next day I had already rejected twelve knockout outfits, put on and taken off so much makeup my nose looked like a rummy's, and straightened and curled my hair till it hurt. I was about to chuck the whole thing when I got an inspiration. I washed my face clean, put the slightest amount of glow-all over my skin, a smidgin of cover-all under my eyes, a hint of blush-all on my cheeks, and some lard on my lips to make them soft. I put on a creamy-white, schoolgirl-like silk shirt over my discreetly bra'd bosom, slid into rather snug blue jeans and riding-type boots, looked at myself full in the mirror, and loved myself so much that for a moment I didn't need Mr. Towns or anybody else.

I was nervous waiting on the street while all the kids came running out of the school. I gave Adam one of the more superior examples of short shrift, and finally Mr. Towns came out. He looked honestly happy to see me. I restrained my mouth until we were seated in a very unromantic coffee shop around the corner from the school. I smiled sweetly a lot, lowered my eyes a lot, and let him talk. He made his point very well, I agreed to everything, and then I hit him with all that good stuff I'd been storing up from *Cosmopolitan* magazine. I asked him some adorable questions about his background and such, and saw to it that my top button opened, showing just the slightest hint of my rather swell cleavage. I stroked my cheek, fingered my hair, and never took my eyes off his.

At some point the game of it all left me, and I started to panic. I felt old and foolish and crazy; no, that's not true, not old— young and very passionate and dizzy and I couldn't hear what he was saying anymore. I was so afraid that I would burst into tears in front of this angel and blow everything for all time. I guess he had stopped talking, and I found myself saying, "I wish we could just go someplace where you could put your arms around me and touch me for a minute or two." He didn't know what to say. I knew that I had to break the silence. I had to think of something that was either very honest and smart or pretty goddamn funny. . . . Nothing. Finally when the silence became unbearable I decided to level.

"Listen, uh—the cat seems to have made off with my tongue, as they say, but I really do have something to say to you which I think will interest you and vice versa. And I'm a little nervous now, but if we could meet again—say tomorrow—I feel I could uh really uh get it all together, as they say. Not me, you understand, I never say things like that but uh meet me, meet me, meet me O.K.? Am I pressing?"

"Where do you want to meet?"

"You mean you will?"

"How about Schrafft's?"

"Insanity, we'd meet all the mothers and their kids there."

"The little pizza place on Ninety-fourth and Madison."

"The smell makes me sick!"

"The Russian Tea Room."

"I know everybody there."

"For Christ's sake we're just going to talk, we're not going to make love on the table!"

"Then I'm not coming!"

"That's not funny."

"It's not supposed to be."

"Yes, it is. Everything you say is meant to be funny."

"O.K. That's fair enough; it seems to be my way of coping

with or delaying the real relationship bit. There's nothing very veiled or devious about this. I'm a slightly older broad who's wildly attracted to you. I've been having a hell of a time playing a game, and now that it's time to put up or shut up, I don't know how to behave. Believe it or not, it's never happened to me before . . . never. A few crushes on movie stars have been the limit of my . . . uh . . . experience. I desperately don't want to be foolish or one of those ladies . . . but I don't think I can bring it off. Maybe I need somebody older or more experienced, who knows the rules, how to get in and out of the Dixie Hotel in twelve minutes . . . Something . . . That's it. We'll go to the Dixie Hotel. Everybody jokes about it, but I never met anyone who's been there. Sensational idea! I knew I'd come up with it. It's this creepy place where all the hookers go, on Forty-third Street. We can meet in the cocktail lounge . . . *The Cocktail Lounge,* I love it! We won't meet a soul and we can talk, and maybe it'll happen, maybe it'll be all right and work out and everything, and maybe we'll like each other a lot. But I'll never get to be a drag . . . never . . . you see I'm really happily married and I love my husband and my kids, and I have a life of my own so I'll never get hysterical and dependent. . . . Well . . . not dependent anyway. And we'll have a good time, oh, I know we will, and we'll laugh and make love . . . and it will be like . . . well . . . sort of like . . . adding . . . a new dimension to our lives which are O.K. already . . . if you know what I mean . . . and I'll never ask questions or pry . . . and I swear . . . I really swear on my kid's head . . . I'll never call you or show up at the school or anything . . . and the best part . . . there'll be no regrets . . . when it's over, it's over . . . we're both mature and we'll use it . . . use it for the best of it . . . both get what we want out of it . . . if you know what I mean . . . no, you don't . . . I don't mean to be crass but that's the thing . . . we both know why we're doing it . . . for the fun, the deliciousness . . . the . . . ummm . . . spirit of it . . . the spirit and the *fucking* . . ." His head jerked forward, his mouth dropped open, and I guess he stifled the gasp. He righted himself a second later. "Say something. I got carried away. You hate me. I've blown it. You're looking at me with too much understanding. Stop it and say something wonderful this minute or I'll drown myself in the reservoir."

"You are an amazing and beautiful woman . . . "

"You're talking too slow. It's going to be bad news."

"It's no news . . . you're just . . . amazing."

"All you've got is bad and humiliating news. I feel it now just like I felt before that it was O.K. to be hanging in here. But now I've shot off my mouth and turned you off. Right? Right. Well, I wasn't lying . . . I never would push myself on you or anybody else. You wanted me for about three and a half minutes and now you don't. O.K. . . . fair is fair, it's my own fault . . . my mouth won't stop . . . I'm famous for it. But I'll tell you something. I'm a hell of a lot more interesting and amusing than the next school mother who'll proposition you is going to be . . . that's for sure."

"That's for sure."

"Good, then let's give it another try tomorrow . . . just to talk and explore the whole thing. I won't carry on, I'll make you laugh. I'll bring dirty pictures."

He eased his body up and out of the booth in one gentle motion. His pained attempt at a smile wouldn't have fooled a kindergarten person.

"I'm sorry . . . but I'm really late . . . for . . . something. I have to go." He grabbed his parka from the hook and went out the door without putting it on. The waitress brought me the check.

EIGHT

In 1969, Leslie, my sister Shirley's daughter, was the first of the four grandchildren to marry. Nobody liked Nat, her intended, especially my mother. His hair started way too low on his forehead. It was dark, wavy, and from another era, as was his mustache. His body was thick. I guess he'd look appropriate in one of those faded immigrant pictures from the turn of the century.

We had a family meeting about the wedding. We couldn't understand "why"—couldn't change "who"—so we had to decide "where." I offered our house in East Hampton. About two years earlier we had bought this magical, eccentric rambling house. It was at the end of a long dirt road that was lined with enormous trees. The house sat on one of the few hills in the town. The hill had been created by a Colonel Weaver when he built the house in the early 1900s, so that he could look over his polo field, which was now our polo field. Since then two other houses had been built there, so polo playing had to be put on the back burner. The house was fake Tudor but genuine fantasy. Some rooms were up two stairs, some down three, it was all

121

From top clockwise, my family: Leslie, Elliot, Robin, Adam, Bonnie, Adolph, Harry, Elaine, Douglas, Shirley, Mama, and me with Amanda.

about secrets and unexpected places. It had rooms that looked sort of normal, and then you'd open what you thought was a closet door, and there would be another whole room with no other access.

When you walked in the front door, you saw a mini-ballroom-size foyer. Straight ahead was Colonel Weaver's triumph—a large living room with a floor-to-ceiling bow window of separate square beveled glass panes. Through it you saw a splendid variety of old, graceful trees with leaves of every color in the green rainbow. They grouped themselves into a proud and endlessly fascinating arrangement, as if they were posing for a stylish photographer. The glass wall faced west and the sunsets gave special shows for us. The sun would filter through the trees, making patterns in the all-white room and on our faces, coloring everything hot orange as it got lower. Outside, the trees became dark purple with the sky just above them dusty pink and then the clear blue of the ceiling of the sky and the strong white of the stars and planets would appear. And I'd want to cry then and I do now—thinking of the beauty and mystery of that time of day in that old house when kids were young and expectations were high and life was a daily gift.

Don't let them tell you that when you're sick each day is so precious. I just want to put in a little negative vote here. Surprise, surprise. Marcus Aurelius and all those good guys tell us that we must live every day as if it were our last . . . well . . . I say —and, you can quote me—live it as if it were somewhere in the early middle. That's when it works.

Clearly that's a subjective picture of the house. I want you to visualize it on the night before the wedding. Hubs and I were in our bedroom, kids were in their funny sort of "wing." My mother was in the guest room, and every member of my immediate family was doubled and tripled up in the rest of the house —two sisters, two brothers-in-law, three nieces, and a nephew— and even though we weren't crazy about you know who, we all had this family sense of being together for an occasion. Daddy was dead and we bonded and closed up the ranks, filled up the space in a not-too-familiar place. We felt some sort of continuity —children of immigrants, cozy in a New England–like environment, waiting for a class-act wedding. I felt as though I had finally made it. I had shaken off Jersey City, Atlantic City, Gypsies, vaudeville, sweat, wrong moves, wrong forks, bad bones, and finally gotten into an Andy Hardy world. Or better still, *The Philadelphia Story.*

The next morning I was awakened by the sound of strange people's voices and movements. It took me a few moments to remember that this was the wedding day, and that the caterers were there bright and early to get this show on the road. I went downstairs and was taken aback by the numbers of people scurrying about and by the frenzy of activity. Liver was being chopped, or at least pummeled, into a nice mound. Napkins, matchbooks, and yarmulkes that said NAT AND LESLIE, AUGUST SOMETHING 1969 were being stacked on the front hall table. In the kitchen, large sweating persons were cooking or heating large sweating foodstuffs. It was hot as hell in there. There were a number of odd-looking metal objects like small trunks standing on their side—propane gas heaters—scattered around. Earlier that week, they had come to store them in the garage which was under the house. Something about them made me nervous, but I was reassured by the smooth-talking "experienced" caterers that they were perfectly safe and anyway (chuckle, chuckle) we're insured (chuckle, chuckle).

It was as if the house had been invaded by very big Munchkins. Upstairs, hair was being teased, perfume was being dabbed, no, splashed, blue and gray eyeshadow was being rubbed in ever so gently, stays were being inserted into collars, cummerbunds were being fastened, "Miz Scarlett, Miz Scarlett, the stuffed cabbage looks absolutely enchanting . . . so don't you worry your pretty little head, it's gonna be the event of the year. I swear!"

My own little girl, Amanda, who was about five, looked like a small saucy angel. She was in a long white cotton Victorian-looking dress. She was tanned, curly-haired, and her big brown

Amanda and Adam on the wedding day.

eyes were shiny and mischievous. My little boy—the same kind of looks and outlook—was in a blue blazer and shirt and tie. They were so happy, running around, visiting all the rooms, helping their cousins, tasting the food, running their hands over the pink tablecloths of the rented tables. Outside, chairs were being set up for the ceremony.

I checked on the bride. She was looking beautiful and serene. It was almost time. The photographer arrived and took a picture of my kids, of the hall table, of the matchbooks. I fussed around. A few guests arrived. Most of them were on chartered buses from New York. "Hey, wait . . . I hear the buses coming up the driveway. Jesus, it's hot. Adam, come on honey, let's see what's going on. Take my hand."

And then there was a thud, a report, a flash of light . . . "Oh, my God, what the hell is going on?" I panicked. I ran out of the house with my son. I saw stars. I saw flames. "Oh, my God, that was an explosion and the house is on fire . . ."

People were just getting off the bus in front of the house. They were dazed. They didn't know what was going on or where to go. I screamed. No, wrong, I never screamed. I said in an unnaturally deep and calm voice: "Where is Amanda?" Someone told me she was with Adolph. I walked up the dirt road a little and watched the bride, my family, my relatives, people, spilling out of the doors, running around in confusion. Someone brought us to our neighbors' house down the road. On the walk there Adam said, "If this is life, I'm not so sure I want to live it."

East Hampton has a volunteer fire department. Its members are summoned from work, the beach, their homes, by a siren that can be heard all over the village. The number of times it sounds depends on the severity of the disaster. It seemed to me that the siren went on for hours. By now it was a major fire. Sun-colored flames and very black smoke on such a clear, sunny day, were eating away part of our shingled roof, wood-crossed stucco, and front door. The volunteers arrived in a fire truck, driven by the manager of the supermarket. Neighbors came to help. Friends who had seen the smoke and found out it was our house arrived. Listen, this was August in East Hampton, the height of the summer season. The huge, huge lawn, the polo field, was now full of wedding guests, friends, the curious, kids. It was like a Fellini movie. The fire was being fought and the band—a hired "three-piece band" hired for the occasion who had seen too many disaster movies—was playing "Climb Ev'ry Mountain" cha-cha-cha, "You'll Never Walk Alone" . . . up tempo. (Of course, one of those "pieces" was an accordion.)

The rabbi was restless because he was due at another wedding back in New Jersey. The poor bride was hysterical. The caterers were divided. Half of them were trying to get their equipment out, but the waitresses were passing out some hors d'oeuvres, cold, of course, to the assemblage. Nat, the beloved groom, was posing for the photographer holding a hose and wearing a fireman's hat. I was still sitting there . . . numb. I didn't cry, although I usually do at the drop of a house.

The afternoon was building to some kind of frenzied pitch. The rabbi announced that the wedding was going to take place right there on the lawn, with the house—jaunty, jolly—burning in the background. He invoked a book of the Old Testament no one had ever heard of, as his precedent.

"And it saith . . . that ifeth . . . the weddingeth don't taketh place quickly after the fire . . . it will be bad luck!" . . .

Bad luck? Bad luck?! Show me where it's written. Who said that? Sure, I say that now. But if you think anyone argued with him, well, they didn't. It seemed bizarre, but then again . . .

So Leslie put her veil back on, Nat reluctantly took off his fireman's hat, the family assembled, and while the accordion sawed away—some Yiddish-flavored song and "I Love You Truly"—they got married. And then, did we cry . . . and laugh . . .

The next summer we lived in a small, compact prefabricated house set up no more than six giant steps away from a swimming pool which had been completed the month before our real house burned down. From the tiny deck of the prefab, or swimming straight ahead, it would be hard to miss the hulking,

FOR RENT ADORABLE NO FUSS COTTAGE
OLYMPIC SIZE POOL
BREATHTAKING VIEW OF RUINS
COLOR TV

burned-out shell. It was an unusual view for the summer. I mean, how would you word the ad if you wanted to rent it?

One night, we were hanging about in our wet bathing suits watching the news on our very small television, when we saw a picture of one of our friends come on the screen. The newscaster's face told you the story before he said a word. His face changed gears, reset its features, cleared its throat. Then everyone knew. Prominent loved man . . . television colleague as well . . . hell of a guy . . . dead, you know?

We were sad and shocked. Bennett Cerf was not someone we saw daily or even weekly anymore, but we had known him a long time. I had worked with him for a number of years on the most watched, glamorous Sunday night game show, "What's My Line?" We wore tuxedos and gowns and every star worth his or her salt and more turned up. And you had to guess who they were. The panelists had blindfolds on, and the stars would disguise their voices. It was fun for the audience and fun to be on and watched by so many people.

Bennett was, first and foremost, a highly successful, powerful and visible publisher. In his early years, he was a literary maverick who helped *Ulysses* get published in the United States. He published many of the most read and talented authors for forty or so years. He was friends with them and with the cream of the cream of the cream. He liked people of accomplishment and talent. He edited joke books, or humor anthologies as they are sometimes called. He told bad jokes, and puns, but he loved genuinely funny people.

One of his best friends was Frank Sinatra. Bennett and his wife, Phyllis, gave glamorous parties for Frank once or twice a year. Sinatra would sing. Other guys would sing. Adolph would sing the songs he wrote. They always had to coax me, but finally I would sing. In front of "the man" himself. I've never been either comfortable or at my best performing in those kinds of party situations.

Adolph and I were reminiscing, when the phone rang. It was Chris, one of Bennett's sons. I was so surprised that I stumbled over even the most obvious and banal condolence phrases. Chris was upset but mannerly, and full of the busy, busy, that takes over after a death.

"I'm so sorry to bother you. I assume you heard about Dad . . . Thank you . . . Yes, yes, it was . . . Yes, he was . . . She's doing very well. Oh well, I guess it hasn't even sunk in yet . . . He was a great guy, I loved him . . . I know, I know . . . Thank you, I'll tell her. Uh . . . we're sitting around here in the country, we are planning to have a service for . . . Dad . . . Tuesday, the chapel at Columbia University, he loved that school . . . There will be eulogies, and Joe Raposo is going to play some of Dad's favorite songs, and Mom was wondering if you would sing at the end of the service . . . I know, who has? . . . Well, their favorite song was 'They Can't Take That Away from Me.' I could get you a copy. It would mean a lot to Mom and to us. He was really crazy about you, and the way you sing . . . I know you did . . . I know it's hard . . . Thank you, thank you . . . I'm going to miss him so much."

I hung up, and if it is true that stomachs are capable of flip-flops, then count mine in.

There wasn't much time for rehearsal. I had never sung this song except late at night in bed along with Fred Astaire as I watched *Shall We Dance?* I took the sheet music along with me to my singing lesson. After twenty minutes of the usual vocal ease and exercises, I pulled it out.

I have studied singing with Keith Davis for years and years. He has prepared me for auditions, performances, records. He has gotten me onstage on nights when my voice seemed completely shot. Keith is a born and inspired teacher. He lives in one of the last great theatrical buildings on Seventh Avenue in the Fifties. It is full of actors, teachers, musicians, and dancers. Its enormous apartments are now divided into odd combinations of rooms. Keith's is one of the oddest. He has what was once the two back bedrooms of a huge apartment. The bathroom is his kitchen *and* bathroom. Last night's dishes are in the sink, groceries under the toilet, a small refrigerator with a hot plate on top of it wedged between the door and the tub, plus hair preparations, normal bathroom stuff, clothes drying, kitty litter box, all jammed in what was once a parlormaid's "convenience." Beyond that is his bedroom, which is darkened and off limits, but once or twice I went in and it too is full, but of the most sophisticated electronic machines, TVs, stereos, and so forth. The lesson room, or the studio, is an average-size room with an upright piano, three machines to clean the air, a daybed, records, and a straight-back chair where the student sits.

Keith is slight, blond, saintly and devilish-looking at the same time. His hair is thinning, and he has developed a tummy, but he sings with clarity, musicality, and strength and he's the best teacher in New York according to me and much better singers.

"Darling, I have never coached for a funeral before. Just sing it. . . ."

"What if I cry in the middle?"

"Well . . . then you'll just cry, won't you?"

"What should I think of while I'm singing? If I think of the lyrics and Bennett, I'll just dissolve."

"Just think of the music and producing a simple musical line. And for God's sake breathe, don't forget to breathe."

I couldn't go in with the rest of the mourners. I was met by the "arrangement person" and shown into the chapel by the side door which led directly to the nave and pulpit "area." It was all wooden, and very simple. I sat alone on a wooden bench facing another wooden bench. The pulpit and the assemblage were to my left. The mourners were beginning to come in. It was hard to see because the pulpit was in the way and you really had to turn around, which seemed wildly irreverent, to sort of stare at the folks as they came in. I had the, by now, crumpled, soggy piece of sheet music clutched in my wet shaking hands. I looked straight ahead and tried to breathe. The coffin was brought in. Frank Sinatra was one of the pallbearers. Joe was playing a medley of Bennett's favorite pop songs on the grand piano brought in for the occasion. I've always had severe stage fright before a performance. Over the years, I have found bizarre methods of lessening it, slightly. I might exercise, shake my hands and legs, vocalize, drink, scream. But I couldn't do any of those things. I could either breathe or faint. I talked to myself:

"Come on, girl, you can do it. Think of something else . . . concentrate . . . Let's see . . . recite a Shakespeare sonnet. O.K., you don't know any. Think of your children, think of your posture, sit up straight, you're almost on the floor, for God's sake. Make your lips turn *up* at the corners . . . *up, up* lips . . . Oh shit I'm nervous . . . Oh God, just get me through this morning, this song and I'll . . . I'll never read the gossip column before page one . . . I'll think before I speak . . . it's beginning."

The eulogies were brilliant. There were so many aspects of this man and his life to be addressed and they were. For the most part, the people who spoke were writers, and good ones. Their reminiscences were specific, clear, poetic, and in a completely appropriate tone. Truman Capote, William Styron, and the gang. Frank didn't speak, but he was terribly moved and he sat in the front row with the family.

Joe got back to the piano, and I heard my musical intro . . . da . . . da . . . da da da da . . . I got up, and went to the pulpit with my shredded music. Tears came and went without dropping. I really was doing this for Bennett, for the family . . . breathe . . .

> *The way you wear your hat*
> *The way you sip your tea*
> *The memory of all that*
> *No, they can't take that away from me . . .*

There was a reception afterward at the Cerfs' beautiful town house. Then I saw what a distinguished, high-talent group had come. The family hugged and thanked me, and I found myself taking bows, that is, acknowledging their praise as if I had just finished a gig at the Copa. I was drinking champagne and stuffing hot cheese puffs down, when Philip Roth came over to me.

"You sang very well. I would think it would be hard, but you were very good. You hit the right . . . tone. I have this idea. First of all, I'd like to book you right now for my funeral. Do you have a set fee?"

I started laughing, people turned around to look at me because my laugh was so honest but hysterical at the same time.

"Actually, I think we could make a lot of money. I'll be your agent, no schlock services, only the best and the brightest. We'll build up a repertoire . . ."

Then we both started making up songs, fees, and people for whom we would do this. Bennett's family came over to see what was going on. We told them and they started laughing too; soon it spread through the whole group. It cleared the air for a bit. And it was right, because Bennett would have laughed more than anyone, and put it into his next humor anthology.

Five years ago it seemed remarkable to walk into a theater on a weekday afternoon, pay no admission, sit down and see and hear Orson Welles, Meryl Streep, Luise Rainer, Garson Kanin, Ruth Gordon, Lillian Gish, and Alger Hiss, for example. That was a tribute to Arnold Weissberger, a theatrical lawyer. Everyone I've mentioned was really his close friend and/or client. The eulogies were short and affecting. Arnold had always worn a fresh carnation in his lapel, and there was a single bright red one on the piano—the only floral decoration.

Today the assault of AIDS is creating an unnatural climate of early death as a way of life. All bets are off—we have no preparation for this. The world of the theater—like the larger world —is suffering incomprehensible losses and our lives are being diminished in unacceptable proportions. I've been to a lot of funerals lately. They're intensely theatrical, better cast, and more stirring than their long-running neighbors on Broadway. They're usually held in a theater or in one of the two preferred funeral homes in New York City.

Young Amos Abrams was an associate on the production of my show *The Madwoman of Central Park West.* At his packed theater "service," there were blown-up pictures of his two dogs on either side of the stage, and an enormous vessel of flowers cut from the grounds around the door of a country house he loved. Musical comedy songs were sung or played on a piano. The anecdotes were hilarious, "campy," inside, and appropriate. It ended with a short film clip of Amos as a piece of crabgrass in a commercial. There was a close-up of his grin, which was like the one on the ubiquitous SMILE emblem. One of the people who helped organize the event was my friend and producer from *Madwoman,* Fritz Holt.

Fritz's memorial was a couple of years later at the Palace Theatre where *La Cage aux Folles* was playing. He was one of its producers and Arthur Laurents was its director. My childhood friend Jerry Herman was the composer. This day, Arthur was the director of one of his closest friends' "celebration," as it was called. "Goddamnit, Phyllis. This time I'm knocked out. I hear about someone almost every day. But I didn't expect Fritz . . . You know he wouldn't tell anyone. He wouldn't get the right help. I told him to call you . . . he was worried about his hair . . . I told him about you and the ice cap and how it seemed to help during the treatments. I think he was about to . . . Jesus . . . you don't need this. You know exactly what I'm talking about."

It was standing room only at the Palace: the companies, crews, musicians, anyone ever associated with Fritz and *La Cage* turned up. All Fritz had wanted was to be an invaluable part of the Broadway theater . . . he was. In every story told, there were lines from plays or quotes from songs . . . the shared language of the theater community. The service was star-studded, well paced. And here's the difference, ladies and gentlemen, between yours and ours. Our caring, closest kin or non-kin are the people who create "shows" for a living, so they know what they're doing.   .

Among the speakers, and players, were Jerry Herman and Jim Pentecost, *La Cage*'s production stage manager, whose first show was none other than *Madwoman*. And last on the program, Arthur came forward to the microphone with that chiseled, erect powerful little body of his, and asked that everyone who had ever been connected with *La Cage* please come to the stage. Hundreds of men and women silently filed up the aisles. The cavernous Palace stage was jammed. He then asked them to sing Jerry's song from the show, "The Best of Times Is Now." The pianist played the introduction, and they started swaying because that's what the music demands, and, in perfect harmony, they sang:

> *The best of times is now*
> *What's left of summer but a faded rose?*
> *The best of times is now*
> *As for tomorrow*
> *Who knows, who knows, who knows?*
>
> *So hold this moment fast*
> *And live and love as hard as you know how*
> *And make this moment last*
> *Because the best of times*
> *Is now, is now, is now, is now.*

I was not connected with *La Cage* except through friendship. So at the end of the song, as people started leaving the theater, I ran up to the stage just to hug my buddies.

"Wouldn't Fritz have been thrilled—standing room only."

We continue the semi-jokes that are going around our little theatrical community.

"Promise me that you won't let So-and-So sing at mine . . . her vibrato is shocking and the poor darling hasn't hit a note on key since Al Jolson sang in whiteface."

"Promise noted and filed. But, you know what you can do for me? If I go before you—which is highly unlikely owing to my celibacy since childhood—but if God decides to play yet another unamusing joke, promise you won't let Mister So-and-So speak. First of all, he's too used . . . I see him at everyone's. And second, he just starts blubbering. He has no taste . . . no control, my dear . . . and, let's face it, he cannot put a sentence together. Let's have specifics. Let's have style. You *will* do those two little things for me, now, won't you?"

So Philip Roth and I were pioneers in the field. And don't think that I haven't made a pact with a friend or two that we would screen out certain "undesirable elements" from each other's funerals.

Michael Bennett was the youngest dancer in the chorus of *Subways Are for Sleeping.* The "celebration" of his life was held at the Shubert Theatre where *A Chorus Line,* which he directed and helped create, was still playing after thirteen years. The orchestra donated its services and played as home movies of Michael as a child, dancing, appeared on a giant movie screen brought in for the afternoon. Everybody who spoke or *did something* had a powerful dramatic effect. They reflected Michael's uncanny style and sense of dynamics. Numbers from his shows were interspersed among tributes from his family, friends, casts, lawyers, agents, producers, and collaborators. Steve Sondheim played and sang, in a voice barely held together, Michael's favorite song, "Move On," from *Sunday in the Park with George.*

The finale was "One" from *A Chorus Line* sung and danced by the entire cast in full costume—top hats, tails, tights, and canes. At the very end, the many mirrors, which form the backdrop of the show, turned around and an enormous photograph of Michael with his arms spread wide from wing to wing appeared. Was it how he would have done it? Was it how he would have wanted it? It was how it needed to be.

Maybe there should be an award in New York for the best memorial service. Please, don't take offense. It could be given at a very private and discreet dinner; no press, no disco music, just a string quartet, the bereaved, and the organizers.

A theatrical tribal rite . . . a cultural salvo . . . the spirituality depends on you. Just as I'm sitting to write about Bob Fosse, the seductive, miniature hunk who was my director and one of my major flirts—the phone rings . . .

"Phyllis, hi, this is ———. We're going to have a little . . . party . . . yes, a party, that's just what Stark would have wanted." Stark was my agent for a very long time. "It'll be at the Ballroom nightclub from five-thirty until seven. . . . There'll be just a few . . . toasts, and then we'll party . . . nothing grim. I know it would have meant so much to Stark for you to be there . . . his mother's gone . . . there's no real family, but us. God, we do go back a long time, Phyllis, a long time. We'd love it if Adolph would come too, even for a few minutes. . . . Oh, thank you . . . it means a lot . . . thanks. See you . . . Tuesday."

Michael's and Bobby's memorials took place within a couple of weeks of each other. Bobby did not die of AIDS. He had a heart attack on a street in Washington, D.C., on his way out of the theater where he had just finished the dress rehearsal of a company of *Sweet Charity,* starring Donna McKechnie, who had once been married to Michael.

Fosse had fictionalized his open-heart surgery and compulsive life earlier in the brilliant movie *All That Jazz.* I had worked with him in a not terrifically well-fated musical, *Pleasures and Palaces,* that he had directed and choreographed. It was the last show, the last score, that the inimitable Frank Loesser wrote. The tryout town was Detroit. We spent twenty hours every day in that theater working on it. Both Bob and Frank, who were small to begin with, seemed to shrink and become more and more enveloped by the smoke coming out of their nonstop cigarettes. After many weeks, just before we were to move to New York for the opening, we closed. It was a cumbersome historical epic that never seemed to come to life in spite of the hard work of such an accomplished group of professionals.

So, once again, this time for Bobby, I was in the dark Palace Theatre on a sunny afternoon, surrounded by colleagues and friends . . . watching another production and trying to get through my numbed head that not only was I never going to get to do another show with that wicked little dynamo, but more important, I was never going to walk into a room, spot him, and feel those particular Fosse, flirting, funny tinglings come over me. During one of my difficult periods, when there was not enough makeup in the world to disguise my drooping, sallow, haunted-looking face, I had gone to dinner at a friend's and Bobby was there. He knew I was ill. He could sense I felt deeply unattractive and was scared. So, of course, he put me on his lap, caressed my face, talked dirty, and made me laugh. Then I found myself telling him a little about my writing, about my woes. He said, "If you want any feedback, I'd love to read it in any form. Hell, I made my bad ticker pay off. I'll turn your book into a musical. It's my kind of subject . . . Doom . . . Death . . . perks me right up."

He kept me on his lap—he had to, I wouldn't move. He made my evening, he lightened my load. When I got home, I sang to my mirror—my best audience—"I Feel Pretty" from *West Side Story.* The mirror simply loved it. After the kind of week it had had, it was happy to see me feeling better.

Bobby's memorial was different from the others. The participants were all writers . . . all male, except for a wonderful female singer who "closed the show." His wife, collaborator, and friend,

Gwen Verdon, and his beautiful daughter Nicole Fosse chose not to speak. We watched scenes from the varied and powerful movies he directed: *Cabaret, Lenny, All That Jazz,* and *Star '80.* We saw him do a dance on the sand in the film *The Little Prince.* And then came the writers with their carefully chosen words.

That fatalism was the engine of his art and his life . . .
—PETE HAMILL

Of all Bobby's dance numbers, my favorite was watching his insecurity and his confidence tango with each other, gliding and dipping across the years.
—HERB GARDNER

He and I played each other Ping-Pong and the winner was to be designated the youngest forever. . . . He and I finally sat down alone over a glass of wine and reminisced about our lives . . . He looked at me with a big smile on his face and said to me so sweetly and sincerely, "It was great, wasn't it?" And Bob won the game. He'll be the youngest forever.
—NEIL SIMON

Bob Fosse established a Theater Scholarship Fund to support the work and education of performing artists of all kinds—dancers, actors, musicians, writers—and, he hoped, to help ensure a future for the living theater that he loved so much.

We have lost so many of our own we're huddling together for warmth, to close up our robbed ranks, to ward off scary things. We're singing louder, making more jokes, and putting on bigger and better events. We want to make sure we mean something . . . don't you see? We're part of the "live theater." We pass things on through *live* performances, and we want our mothers and fathers, sisters, brothers, and childhood friends whom we left behind, who are stunned, saddened, perplexed, and mourning in the Everyplace-else way, to know that it was worth our leaving Everyplace-else, U.S.A., to come to Broadway.

NINE

Every time I try to tell you about my mother I get waylaid. I get on to other things. This is not a case for Superanalyst, this is not indicative of anything but the difficulty of making sure that you see her, and know her. I want to bring her back to real life, not literary life. I want her here now with her skin and shape and hair and hands. I want her to be sitting at the edge of my bed because I need her advice. Now I really need her advice. I want her to tell me *my future*. I want her to take my hand in hers, turn it over, and stroke the lines in the palm. I want her to stretch out my fingers and feel them and the mound between my thumb and my first finger, and study my hand as if she were reading a rich relative's will without her glasses. Then I want her to speak.

I can't summon her voice. I've turned her into a few memories, some anecdotes, and an unspecific longing. I would love it if you could stand in the hallway of our apartment with me and peek into Amanda's darkened room as my mother sings the old torch songs to my just quieted baby, like the Shirley Temple of grandmothers that she was. You should understand the com-

Mama and me.

plicated feelings both she and I had then about my new "life-style" with Adolph. She knew that I loved her, but that I was still embarrassed about her "profession," her lack of education, and what I perceived as *her* lack of sophistication, but was *mine*. Well, that's from the picture "Everybody Else's Parents Are Colorful." She felt shy . . . from the book "We're the Same Person." She never wanted to intrude. She was in awe of these "famous swells" and the "publicized life" . . . and yet, being the completely, I can't help it, all-knowing seer of seers, she saw the flaws, the weakness, and the fakery. It didn't matter to her . . . she just couldn't bear a sense of superiority without goodness or love. It was only in the last ten years of her life, after Daddy was gone, that I eased up about including her in our private world. I worried that she might be hurt. I worried that some might be contemptuous. I was wrong. Everyone was attracted to her. She told them things that astounded them. I guess I simply have to get my last memory of her out of the way so that I can get past it, go backward, something. I'll tell you fast.

In 1976, I was playing the central character in a play I had also directed called *Walking Papers* by Sandra Hochman. It was produced by Circle In The Square, but we were rehearsing and playing in a dingy, dark space they called a theater in the Martinique Hotel on Thirty-second Street and Broadway. It was and is a welfare hotel. It was Depressing City, and the work wasn't going too well either. The play was based on Sandra's book about a talented woman who often pushed aside her own creative and sexual needs in order to be a "suitable partner" to a series of eccentric and often abusive men. The book was good but it was never successfully theatricalized. It had a fine score by Gary Friedman. I would work on rewriting the script with Sandra at night, go to the theater and direct and stage the rest of the cast and then put myself into it. I felt in control of everything but my performance.

Ted Mann, one of the founders of Circle In The Square, a sharp and seasoned professional, came to a run-through. He told me everybody was doing fine, and that I had directed with a sure and imaginative style, but my character was murky, general, and unsatisfying. He advised me to concentrate on nothing but my acting for a while. That was hard. I wanted to fix everything else, every piece of staging, every note of music. But I forced myself to be "just an actress," while he sat in the audience and watched and helped me. We had a short limited run. Because of the talented people involved, we got full and "important" theatrical audiences. As always, once there were bodies—faceless, because of my nearsightedness—out there, my misgivings fled, and I enjoyed trying to be that other lady.

At every performance, there were friends and family. One night my cute, cute little mother came. She was a twentieth-century baby, born in February of 1900. So she was seventy-six, and blonder than ever. She was wearing a taupey-colored wool cape that flung itself around her neck. She was carrying an old lynx coat of mine. One of her "ladies" fixed furs, so she had this old ratty coat of mine transformed into a fluffy jacket, completely relined in red silk. I saw her excited little face as I came up from the dungeon dressing room. We kissed and hugged, she had tears in her eyes, her usual tears of pride in her baby. I knew she knew the limitations of the material, but she said, "You were so wonderful. You made me cry at the end. Very good people, nice music. I don't quite get the story. Why did she go with those men in the first place? But a lot of it was clever."

Then she showed me the coat, which she had kept on her lap all through the show. She was so pleased as I made a fuss over it, and joked about her "ladies"—her ladies who could get World Series tickets, when no one else could, who would come and pick up Adolph and the kids and me, when we needed to get to Jersey, before we had a car, who cooked or brought her food, who worshiped her and us as her extension. Her adoring "ladies" and their secret lives. We never quite knew who they were or just how she had obviously changed their lives. We only knew that when we tried to thank them for any one of these diverse favors, they all said, "Oh, please, I'd do anything for that mother of yours, that Mrs. Newman . . . what a woman. She saved my life."

After the show a small family group went to a big delicatessen on Sixth Avenue between Thirty-fourth and Thirty-fifth streets. Please note the location, because I note it every time I'm driving uptown on Sixth Avenue. I note it . . . and I look away and go into one of my countless, daily minitrances.

It was a Jewish delicatessen. And even back then, our consciousness had been raised or lowered enough so that we talked endlessly about diets, fats, weight, and then ordered hot pastrami sandwiches. My mother held hers up as if to toast our warm and tight and happy little group. She was the heart and soul of our shared joy. Then I saw her slip cash under the table to Adolph, as she had done all her life with my father. He didn't want to take it, but she insisted. It was her party. My sister and brother-in-law laughed and shook their heads. And maybe it's because of what happened after, that I think I never felt as much love and admiration for her as I did right then, right there.

A few nights later I was having a closing-night cast party at our apartment. Those parties are filled with mixed sentiments. Whatever the experience has been, you have made instant intimate attachments. It was about midnight. We had finished eating our lasagna, we were drinking a lot of wine and trading rehearsal stories, singing songs that were cut out of the show, letting our collective hair down. The phone rang, Adolph answered it. When he came in, his face had that layered look. I got on the phone with my sister Shirley.

"Momma didn't want me to tell you until tomorrow. She didn't want you to be upset. But I think you should know. She's in the hospital. Nothing serious. Really, honey."

(Now she starts crying, she can't help herself. Momma hasn't been in a hospital since I was born. Momma doesn't go to doctors. If Momma went to a hospital, it is serious, and Momma knows in her way, the spooky way, the real way, that it's serious.)

I never went back to the party. The news filtered through. A few of the people came up to say good night and wish my mother well, and within five minutes everyone left. I know this sounds melodramatic; after all everybody goes to the hospital all the time. But not in my family. My father went into the hospital once—about ten years earlier—and three days later he died. Same hospital. Same month of the year.

The next morning I drove to Jersey City to the hospital. I was so terrified and so certain that this was the beginning of the scene from my life called the "The Death of My Beloved Mother." I was acting it out, don't you see? I was preparing every second of the forty-five-minute drive. I started to grieve, to mourn. I never thought a good thought, or what they now call a positive thought. I was protecting myself. I was pretending it had happened, and I'd gotten through it. When I arrived at the dreaded hospital of my father's death, my sisters and one of my mother's good friends were very optimistic. One doctor, they said, was gloomy and didn't know what was wrong, but he thought it was critical. A new doctor didn't know what was wrong, but he thought it probably wasn't critical.

I went into my mother's room, and she was in good spirits. She was joking. She was encouraged by our faces reporting the latest news. But she had a very strong feeling. She said, "I wish they would operate."

"But, Mom, no one is even mentioning that."

"I know, and you know me and operations, but I wish they would. I think that would be the right thing."

I won't go on with this, just know that she was right. They

never did anything for her. By the time we tried to move her to a New York hospital three days later, it was too late. Adolph and I waited in the ambulance entrance at Mount Sinai Hospital that morning for hours. Finally we called, and found out that she wasn't going to arrive. We rushed to Jersey City, we took the children. Her doctor had finally called in a God-knows-what specialist. My mother looked terrible, her stomach was distended, there were black particles coming through the clear liquid in the tubes in her nose and I don't know where else. She was sweet, she was afraid, she still wanted them to operate.

We all gathered in a waiting room, while the "specialist" looked at her. Then we heard the piercing sound of the red alert. Nurse, aides, oxygen, wheels, shoes, bodies, rushed by to the room, her room. We all stopped talking, we breathed in a whole new rhythm. We held hands. I could not look at my children, or anybody for that matter.

The "specialist" walked in the room. A man we had never seen until twenty minutes before was going to tell me that my precious mother was dead. At that moment my son Adam, who was fifteen, said it for all of us: "Oh fuck . . ."

Neither Adam nor I, nor most people, spoke like that then. It was startling. What a terrible thing.

Now, I'm going to tell you a wonderful thing. On her next to last day, she and Adolph and I had been alone in the room. She was still cheerful. She had the all-too-familiar tubes, but her eyes were not haunted, I promise you. She took my hand, nondramatically looked at me, and really smiled . . . absolutely not your stock deathbed smile . . . and said, "You're going to be all right. You really are." Isn't that something—some mother? She didn't say, "Don't worry, *I'm* going to be all right." She just said the *future truth*. For the first time, she told my fortune.

That exemplary, humorous, psychic, lively, loving, loyal peach of a mommy gave me that gift. And, of course you know that during the tough times of my own physical truth, somewhere, someplace, like right behind my eyebrow, I knew the psychic truth too.

I know I've told you a lot of laughing-on-the-outside-crying-on-the-inside stories . . . but what do you want me to do? Invent another life? Well, I would if I could and sometimes I do.

Gloria Jones, the widow of the great writer and our beloved friend James Jones, speaks completely without guile or fore-thought. I mean this in the best sense. She says what people think before they edit what they say.

When I found out about the first, she was the only one to say: "Shit, does that mean they're going to lop it off? Holy Mother of God . . . I hope you won't die . . . This is so terrible. . . . You are some number, I'd be fainting."

When Gloria heard about the second one: "Christ, how terrible. I'm so sorry. Jesus, talk about flat-chested . . . what about sex? . . . Well, you can always back into the guy!"

This looks crass on paper, but you have to picture her—blond, big-bosomed, generous in body and spirit. She's not young, not old, a lived-in Marilyn Monroe type, hostess, innkeeper, mother to her two children and to any who come by, if you pass her test: "Are you genuine? Genuinely interesting, genuinely talented. Or a fabulous faker? Do you have a problem? Are you having a party? Will you have a little drink with me? . . . Well then, I'm so happy to see you. This is a beautiful party. Aren't you wonder-ful . . . " She's neither pretentious nor silly, she knows a lot. The information comes out staccato-like, no flowers, the facts correct, the theories original . . . truth.

"Well, you're alive, and that's good!"

Yes, that's very good. She is right.

When her husband died, Gloria, constantly surrounded by loving friends, lay on the couch holding the top of her rib cage under her large left breast with her thumb stretched as far as it could toward the back, and the rest of her fingers outstretched and stiff. It was as if she were measuring the pain in her heart. And she was. There was always a Scotch with a little bit of soda nearby. Every so often she would look up at whoever happened to be sitting with or near her and she would say, "That didn't happen . . . did it? Jim didn't really die . . . did he?" I never heard anyone answer her.

For quite a while after my mother's death I didn't spend much time off my bed. My bed is command central even in the best of times. I got off for the occasional job at that time, but little else. My career was in a nondefinable state of semiconsciousness. Every so often, I would shake it the way you shake a dozing senior citizen. "Huh? Huh? I'm awake . . . I'm working . . . projects . . . not enough women's parts . . . I don't want to move to California . . . I'm writing . . . I'm directing . . . I'm changing . . . My kids . . . my husband . . . my standards . . . my age . . . ZZZZZ."

On one phone call, I was moanin' low with jokes to Steve Sondheim. He was telling me about a trip that he was going to take with Judy and Hal Prince to a musical theater seminar and conference in Sydney, Australia. They had been invited along with Alan Jay Lerner. One of the inducements was a round the world airplane trip. Hawaii, Fiji, Hong Kong, New Delhi, and so forth, and back home through London. He got me invited along. I gave classes on musical comedy acting and singing, I sang Steve's songs on a TV show with Steve at the piano, and, incidentally, I saw the Taj Mahal. I got to mourn in a majestic way that befit a mother like that. Steve is known among his friends as a generous and creative gift giver. This was, possibly, the most thoughtful and profound one he has ever given.

When I came back from Australia I wanted to perform desperately, but I really didn't know how or where to put myself. I felt different. I felt empty and full at the same time. I wanted to express myself, I needed to deal with my loss and move on.

I got a call from a nightclub called the Grand Finale, on the Upper West Side of New York City, which was building a reputation as a good showcase for theater people and their acts. I said yes and picked a date, knowing that the deadline would force me into some kind of creative action. The first thing you need when you're putting a musical evening together is a gifted and inventive musical conductor and arranger. I called Steve Sondheim for suggestions. The first name he offered was Glen Roven. He was, he said, a young man with talent and credentials.

I arranged to interview him, and I was surprised, to say the least, when a small kid walked in. He was seventeen and looked twelve. It was difficult for me not to act like his mother. So I compromised and treated him like my son.

He was fast talking, knew everything, and was more of a smart ass than I am. When he got to the piano he was home. He simply knew every song that had ever been written, and if he didn't, he'd fake it. He was filled with ideas and enthusiasm. I told him that it may seem pretentious as hell, but I wanted to . . . well, almost assess myself, my mother, women who had influenced me, my family, and do this in a fun-filled hour on a nightclub stage. He didn't flinch, but, of course, he was just a kid, what did he know?

For years I had been listening to the lyrics of certain popular songs about women and I realized what a really strong and stereotypical influence they had and have on impressionable types like me. They helped fill out that big picture of the American second sex. I told this to Glen, and we started trading and discovering those songs. We decided to do a medley of them—a "Women's Medley."

When I have a brand new hair-do
With my eyelashes all in curl
I float as the clouds on air do
I enjoy being a girl . . .

The girl that I marry will have to be
as soft and as pink as a nursery . . .

            (In French accent in a leering Chevalier manner)
Thank heaven for little girls
'cause little girls get bigger every day . . .

I flip when a fellow sends me flowers
I drool over dresses made of lace

I talk on the telephone for hours
With a pound and a half of cream upon my face!

The moment I wake up
Before I put on my make up
I say a little prayer for you . . .

Homework . . . I wanna to homework . . .
instead of an office, I wanna work home . . .

She may get weary, women do get weary
Wearing the same shabby dress
When she gets weary
Try a little tenderness . . .

I'd be so happy to keep his dinner warm
As he goes onward and upward
Happy to say good evening dear
I'm pregnant . . .

                    (Glen sings)

You're having my baby
What a wonderful way of saying how much you love me . . .

                    (I sing)

I'm having his baby
I'm a woman in love and I love what it's doing to me . . .

                    (Band sings)

Everybody ought to have a maid . . .

          (Me with babushka, bowing and scraping)

La . . . la . . . la . . .

                    (Band sings)

Someone who's efficient and reliable, obedient, pliable . . .

(I sing)

Capable, pliable women, women
Undemanding and reliable
Knowing their place . . .

There is nothing like a dame . . .

Women are irrational, that's all there is to that
Their heads are full of cotton, hay and rags
They're nothing but exasperating, irritating, vacillating
Agitating, calculating, maddening and infuriating hags . . .

He is pleased with me
My lord and master . . .

I am woman, you are man
I am smaller
So you can be taller than . . .

A woman is a sometime thing
I say a . . . woman . . . is . . . a . . .

Tits and ass
Tits and ass have changed my life . . .

					(And then the resolution)

So do not push me, shove me, turn me around
'cause I'm no one's toy
You can charm me, chase me, follow me home
I won't be coy
You may not like it much
But I'm my own great joy
And not some sugar and spicey lacey and nicey
Cutie you're going to enjoy
No . . . I'm no one's toy!

The last song which framed the whole medley was originally sung by Raggedy Ann in a musical by the talented Joe Raposo. We took it, with Joe's approval, and used it as a woman's self-recognition, rather than that of a soft doll.

That medley became the focal point of the act. We knew that it would come at the climax of the evening, and we had to work toward it. We couldn't just hammer home a message, we also had to have good songs that were not necessarily pertinent, because nightclub acts were not the inevitable starting place for feminist musicals.

As the act started taking shape, I called in my friend Arthur Laurents. His body of work as a playwright, screenwriter, librettist, novelist, and director is like no one else's. He's skillful, serious, outrageous, wildly funny, political, original, tender, tough, and universal.

He listened and guided us. He suggested a young dancer and choreographer, Tony Stevens, to come in and stage it. Tony brought another layer of imagination. For example, the "Women's Medley" is a fairly long piece of material with both a dramatic and comedic line, so it needed subtle and appropriate staging. One day, Tony brought a large square cotton scarf to rehearsal. He told me to try using it during the number and we'd see what happened. That scarf gave both of us the visual core and the key to the character changes in the medley. I started out using it like a stripper's feather boa. Then it became a teenager's hanky, a rolled-up ball to make a larger fist, a dust rag, a Kleenex taking off makeup, an apron, a maternity dress, a babushka, a shawl, and then finally it got thrown away, symbolizing . . . well, you know.

The final act was a small revue. I was pleased that it contained both substance and whimsy.

Like all opening nights it was filled with tension. I hadn't played a club for a long time. One of the dizzying fears is that I'll mess up the lyrics and/or music of the writers who are sitting in the audience. In a small club, even with my Magoo-like vision, I can see them and feel them. I often have one of my fabulous conversations with myself before such evenings and audiences.

"Now see here, Phyllis. You are doing this show for the audience, for yourself, not for Adolph or Cy or Steve or Lenny. Right? Sure. Or for Jule or Richard Rodgers's daughter or Oscar

As you can see, I'm an emotional singer.

Hammerstein's son or Cole Porter's ghost. Lighten up . . . stop obsessing."

That does its usual no good. My only salvation is getting up and doing it. It went very well. Afterward in my dressing room, Arthur L. said, with his special type of conviction and enthusiasm, that he thought the act was the basis for a whole show, a one-woman show. I always take what Arthur says very seriously.

A young man named Craig Anderson was at that time the artistic director of the Hudson Guild Theatre. It is an off-off-Broadway, tiny perfect theater in the middle of a housing development and community center in the West Twenties. Craig had been having a couple of impressive seasons with new plays and innovative scheduling. Arthur had told him the possibilities he perceived for my show. Craig had never seen the act, so I arranged to be part of a concert series at Town Hall. I got everything and everyone together for that one night. There was a big audience, but I was really doing it as an audition for one attractive young blond fellow named Craig. He liked it, but we both knew it needed to be transformed from a nightclub act with storytelling moments into a written, structured play with music.

We met with Arthur who said he would certainly help and advise. He suggested that I start writing it. Craig then did something for which I will be eternally grateful. He scheduled "Untitled Show with Phyllis Newman" as the last show of the very season we were in. Giving me, us, a deadline of about six months. It was nuts, and that's why it happened.

The first thing I wrote was an imaginary dialogue with my daughter who was then about thirteen. We were having the classic mother-daughter confrontations at the time, and I thought that a highly stylized, mostly fictional scene about that could be funny, revelatory and easily identifiable, whichever end you were on.

WOMAN

I'm going to start the day with a bang.

(Vamp begins and plays under the following)

(She crosses to the bed, picks up small weights—lifts them once—throws them down; crosses to her vanity and picks up a bottle of vitamin pills, then crosses to the scale to check her weight. When she sees what it is, she throws the pills away and crosses to bed and picks up pad and pencil. She sits cross-legged on the bed and sings:)

Get pajamas for the children
Get a hundred postage stamps
Get a painter, get a pap test
Get a list of summer camps . . .

(Door knock)

(to audience): It's my daughter.

(Toward door)

Go away, I'm functioning.

(Back to list)

Get the handyman to fix the leak
Get Hertz and Rent-a-Car

(Music stops)

All right, all right. Enter. Yes, you are disturbing me, but if it's that important, lay it on me. Are you finished? . . . Surprise. I am genuinely going to be calm about this. Rational. Fanciful, even. I am going to pretend that I am speaking to a real person instead of a demented thirteen-year-old.

Oh, honey, would you please wipe off that eye makeup. It's the wrong kind, it's all smudged and it's mine.

O.K.?

Not O.K.

Let's get one thing straight. Woman to . . . kid. I am not the town dumping ground and I emphatically reject your premise that every time some goon friend of yours cuts you dead . . . every time you get a lousy grade, every time your face breaks out . . .

It is all simply because *I* am the Madwoman of Central Park West and I have filled you with loony genes!

That is precisely what you said! And I emphatically deny it!

Don't, don't, don't, don't you turn on the TV. Look at me.

I'm extremely well organized. When I suffer a little setback, a little breakdown, I don't lay it on my mother; I work it out for myself.

Which happens to be what I am in the middle of doing right now, trying to make everything work.

Look, look, at all these lists. Have you ever heard of a *really* crazy lady who made so many lists?

Why can't I make up my mind about what? Whether I am a normal mother or a quasi-actress?

What do you mean "quasi"?

Don't push me too far. Sit down. I said *put it there*. Now you listen to me. I have played this mother routine by all the rule books. Not because anyone put a gun to my head but because I enjoy it. It comes naturally. I think I'm pretty good at it and so does your brother . . . of course he's older! I'm a normal mother. First you have a son, then you have a daughter.

What? . . . what's not normal? That you haven't had thirteen *theme* birthday parties? You've had 324 sleepovers in the last six days . . . and on the 7th you rested, not me!

Yes, you're absolutely right; this is getting us nowhere!

Which is where I am anyway.

(Sound of door slam)

(She writes furiously)

"Send the kid to boarding school."

(Toward door)

You're not allowed to watch television for the rest of your natural life!

(Laughing)

I like that. That's a good one. You know what I need? I need a file box for my snappy retorts. That's it, that's it *(Writing):* "Get file box for snappy retorts."

That kid's never going to catch me empty-mouthed again. "Quasi-actress!"

(Calling)

Quasi-child!

(Writing)

"Do not be deeply affected by your child. Remember you were one."

One what?

All jokes aside, I've got to clean up this room.

(Writing)

"First: clean up this room."

Make your bed and then, lie in it. *(Music starts)* And then get out of it? *(Music up slightly louder)* It wasn't supposed to be like this . . .

(Phone rings)

MACHINE: Don't hang up. If you wish to speak to the little man, call back after six. If you wish to speak to the little darlings, look them up in the Yellow Pages under "Overprivileged." Please leave your name and number when you hear the beep and you will get a full tank of unleaded gas.

Above all, do not have a good day.

I took a rough version down to Arthur's house. I also took a record of a song I had just heard on the radio. It was called "Copacabana." I thought it was funny and unusual and I wanted Arthur to hear it. From that meeting on, a strong but as yet undefined collaboration started.

Arthur was an expert on structure. I jotted down everything he said. The process of writing a show, like writing anything else, is terribly difficult to describe. At some point we became coauthors. We took separate sections of the show and wrote them alone and then we would meet and work on them together. When the time came . . . we had a show.

It was called "My Mother Was a Fortune-Teller."

We started rehearsals with Craig Anderson directing. One day during rehearsal, Arthur came in and said, "I can't get that song 'Copacabana' out of my head." (By this time the song was a tremendous hit.) "Let's see what we can do with it."

He handed me a chair and I started singing. I tried sitting, I tried imitating Barry Manilow, whose hit it was, but nothing seemed to illuminate it or make it funnier, my own, or part of the antic story I wanted to tell. Then Arthur told me to turn the chair around and sit with my legs astride, like Marlene Dietrich in *The Blue Angel*. I did. And a character started emerging—a combination of Marlene, Lotte Lenya, all Brecht-Weill ladies, and a little Fanny Brice and Erich Von Stroheim. I sang with a low German accent, telling and yelling the story of Lola the show girl and Tony and their tragic end at the Copa. Arthur's ideas for staging were insane. *We* laughed so hard during all the rehearsals we were sure it was going to die in front of an audience.

What makes it all worthwhile? You're so far ahead of me. When the first audience finds it even funnier . . . and their laughs, in unexpected places, help you to shape a comic entity. The show opened to extremely good reviews and reaction and was optioned for Broadway by a trio of producers who had real faith and vision to bring this odd (for then) piece to commercial audiences. Fritz Holt, Barry Brown, and the beautiful Gladys Rackmil all went on to produce many things, but none, probably, that was as risky.

It took over a year and a half to get the backing, the right setup, and all the things it takes to put on a Broadway show. During this time, Arthur and I rewrote it, he retitled it "The Madwoman of Central Park West," and we asked some of our friends and the best composers and lyricists of the theater to contribute songs. They were asked to write a specific song for a particular scene in the show. Everyone agreed. Adolph, Betty, and Lenny wrote an unusual and brilliant opening number called "Up, Up, Up." It accurately describes how much self-approval this character needs to begin another day.

Arthur and I went to see Fred Ebb and John Kander, the songwriting team who wrote, among other things, the powerful score for the musical *Cabaret,* and described the second scene in the show, in which the woman goes to a seminar, a mixture of est and other self-help confrontational groups that were so popular in the seventies. The woman gets up to "share," but as she starts telling her story, she is challenged by the "leader" (in our show a voice over the sound system). He says she's insincere, just a showoff looking for cheap laughs. We needed to musicalize the layers underneath her wisecracking, smart-ass exterior. Fred and John asked a lot of questions about the character and about me. I told them about my being a cheerleader in high school.

A few weeks later they called us and asked us over. They shyly said they just might have a glimmer of an idea . . . well, sort of a rough number. We sat and listened to Fred sing—with John at the piano—an entire story in words and music about a cheerleader named Peggy, an enthusiastic young girl who married

her adorable childhood sweetheart, had two perfect kids, cheered them all through illness and money problems and growing up, and then found herself with not much left to do when they were grown up. She winds up on lithium in a hospital. When her husband comes to visit her, she says, "Bob, I remember what the cheers were . . . but tell me . . . what was all the cheering for?"

There was also a mostly unknown song called "Don't Laugh," that was written by Steve Sondheim and Mary Rodgers for Judy

Holliday in her last show, *Hot Spot.* The show had not been successful, but Judy was as always, wonderful. Nobody knew that during the show she was dying. Adolph had taken me up to visit her in the hospital after her mastectomy, before the show had gone into rehearsal. She looked very sick. There were no fake jollies. I was much younger, it scared me profoundly.

I don't much feel now like describing the song, or the show, or show business . . . I think I need to riff on Judy for a while. I'll do it silently . . . without you. There'll be other shows, there'll be other good times.

At the moment, all I seem to remember are the moments when I got bad news. I can't remember an authentically happy moment, surely there were some, a few. I'm a real laugher, folks. I never stop. I laugh when I'm happy (in theory), I laugh when I'm nervous, I laugh to fill up spaces and empty places. And I laugh a lot alone in the bathroom when I look at my mutilated body, and make up macabre, but funny, songs and monologues.

The night before the second taking of the breast . . . my breast . . . I looked at my woeful, left-behind, drooping, scarred, re-maining, pathetic right breast and started singing: "You were just one of those things . . . just one of those crazy things . . . one of those tits, that now and then rings . . . etc. etc."

O.K. . . . O.K. So it isn't the height of wit, maybe slightly taste-less. Noel Coward would have said it better, but he didn't have to. Cole Porter—he lost a leg—I wonder if he did good jokes or lyrics about that? I'll have to look it up. Where? *Gray's Anatomy?* Or Stanley Green's *Encyclopedia of the Musical Theatre?*

My mother was a fortune-teller
Here's my fortune she told
You'll sing and dance and make the people happy
Everything you touch will turn to gold

All men will want you
You can pick and choose them
Someday you'll find your prince

He'll be rich and handsome
And he'll love you always

Oh I've thought a lot about it since
Yes, I've thought a lot about it since

My mother was a fortune-teller
Who predicted my fate
Was to be an artist who would use her talents
Someone clearly destined to create

With a sense of humor
And a sense of values
Full of goodness full of cheer
Love of God and country
Dogs and cats and children

What would she say now if she were here?
What would I say now if she were here?

My mother was a fortune-teller
And though most of it came true
I am still surprised if someone doesn't love me
Or if something that I did won't do

But I sing and dance and try to make you happy
Turn disasters into jokes
Stay with the man I married, and my dogs and children
But you ain't heard nothin' yet, folks
No, you ain't heard nothin' yet, folks

'Cause my mother was a fortune-teller
Yes my mother was a fortune-teller
Oh my mother was a fortune-teller

(Spoken)

The funny part is, she really was.

TEN

I don't remember how it felt to get dressed when I was a little, little girl, but it couldn't have been so easy. My first memory was how hard it was to close skirts over my big tummy when I was nine. At thirteen, or twelve maybe, I didn't quite know how to handle those budding breasts, so dressing time was upped by a few minutes while I looked at them, held things tight across them to see the effect, and fiddled with stolen bras of my mother's which were ninety sizes too big. A few years later, dressing time again escalated as I tried to turn my thin, dark head-to-toe person into June Haver, June Allyson, or June Preisser. I copied their clothes exactly, I studied their mannerisms in front of my bathroom mirror . . . but even after an hour and a half of dressing, I came out dark and me.

In the late fifties, the New Look and very straight sheaths were the thing. I wrestled with my conscience and girdles, to turn ample hips into an acceptable silhouette. I lost, but not before I had clocked golden overtime, dressing and undressing in a series of bathrooms. Twice in the sixties I was happily pregnant and fat, fat. I was working daily and nightly on television, so the Lord, my husband, and my producer forgave me for wasting so much time dressing to look acceptable to an unsuspecting and then suspecting audience.

I had some good years. I was in a series of musicals on Broadway, my weight was down, and I had people to dress me at the theater, and best of all I had characters to assume, and clothes brilliantly designed for those characters. I felt confident. In *The Apple Tree* I played a different character in each of the three acts. I was made and re-made-up, coiffed, dressed, undressed endlessly. I made one complete change in thirty seconds almost in view of the audience. All I had to do was relax, pull off one wig, and let the experts do it to me. So, my at-home bathroom dressing was down to five minutes . . . shower, jeans, no makeup. Now, we're talking the great years.

Around forty came a new wrinkle, so to speak. Do I dress like a youngish elegant lady or an old girl? Do I throw away the Indian jewelry? Do I replace denim with gabardine? Should I put on a real dress? Do I stop shopping in the junior departments? Should I pull my hair back? Should I cut it or just eat a peach? Should I aim for Diane or Buster Keaton? I spent days locked in my bathroom . . . looking for a look. I'd come out only to eat and work. I would say I missed most of the social events of the seventies while I was trying to get dressed for them. My hubs danced alone for a decade. Finally, the erratic eighties arrived. The years of women, priorities, nonconformity, loose clothes—it's what's inside that counts. The years of Sissy Spacek, Meryl Streep, Yentl (for God's sake), Jane Fonda's leotards—as long as you work out, it works.

Then along came . . . well, you know what . . . and on the road to recovery I now had to get over a new self-imposed obstacle: costume fittings for my first job after the surgery. I was ashamed, as if I had done a bad thing. Those fittings are usually easygoing affairs—you stand around in your underwear or not, while males and/or females try things on you, hold things up to you, stitch and drape things.

I took the sweet young woman who was assisting me aside and

whispered garbled half-sentences. "Uh, surgery . . . Privacy . . . Help myself . . . Bathroom." And off I went to my safe place. I made forty trips back and forth during the hour or so I was there. The male designer must have thought I was a loon. I was sweating but the dresses looked good. No one could tell the difference.

At the theater, I dressed myself every night, only allowing the dresser in to zip up the last few inches. I never took my robe off in case someone came in. I was worried when I had to hug my leading man, but he was so nervous, he didn't even notice. Then I went on tour with my own one-woman show. I played universities and arts centers, one-night engagements. Often my dressing room was a classroom, or student dressing room. There were no locks. I devised an elaborate method. I was alone in a huge empty room, usually with two doors. I would hang a gown or dress on each of the doors. In case anyone walked in without knocking, the falling of the hanger would alert me and I could cover myself. Also that meant twenty-seven insane explanations in twenty-seven nights to twenty-seven young people assigned to dress me.

I got my professional getting dressed down to a neurotic inexact science. My home-life/social dressing time was still monumental. Discarding favorite low-necked sweaters and dresses bugged me. I had definitely been from the "If you've got them flaunt them" finishing school. I spent hours draping scarves over borderline tops. Getting undressed and putting on a nightgown turned into a three-act drama.

Every week for six months I had to figure what to wear and how to get dressed for my chemotherapy treatments. I wanted to go right from bed, carried in a robe with clown white on my face. But I couldn't. People recognized me.

One time my doctor asked me to see a new patient of his. She was a beautiful young television newscaster who was just starting her treatments. I had dressed and made up snappily. My hair looked fine and was there, what's more. I think and hope I helped her. One publicly visible person reassuring another that we could keep on trucking.

"I'm not an evangelist. But I've had four months of this disgusting stuff. I've never missed a performance, show, or a truly hot date. My hair is O.K. I have not gained weight. I have not had the dreaded nausea to a degree that it was even remotely unbearable. I'd sell my soul not to be going through all this. But you know what? I'm fine, I really am now, and will be fine. And so will you. I'd never lie to another woman."

It had been a big day, getting dressed for the celebration of the end of the six months of treatment. Let's face it, I was so relieved that I hurled on my rubber thingie, dressed almost normally, and once again got on with it. For a couple of months . . . and then numero duo. All right . . . two thingies. But now I got to choose my "look." I chose small and boyish. I felt I had earned an entire, new, expensive lot of apparel, but I didn't feel like trying anything on, and I was sick of the disguising caper. I bought two oversized hot-colored jackets and that was it. Except it wasn't. I'd still fantasize over *Vogue* magazine, imagine I was going to look like them, like that, like her. I'd wait until ten minutes before we were due somewhere. I started despising those same two jackets and the hundreds of earrings of fake bright-colored stones I had bought in the mistaken notion that they would lighten my face, my attitudes and my soul.

No more hearts and flowers. This is it. Get dressed fast and don't look. No, I'm not going to have reconstruction, I wouldn't know what to do with them anymore. Anyway, by that time I'd grown accustomed to my spaces.

One night I watched myself on Johnny Carson. I was dressed in a bright blue satin big jacket borrowed from Jean Kennedy Smith. I noticed, when they came in for a close-up, something new. A "thing" on my face between my eyebrows. A month later, it's back to the bathroom mirror and the drawing board. It was a large basal cell carcinoma—skin cancer. Its removal left a one-inch angry red scar; no, that's too gentle and too familiar a description. There was an apoplectic, Day-Glo crimson stigma dead center from the top of my eyebrows down to the beginning of my nose. Getting dressed now involved flesh-colored tape bisecting that spot, but the red spilled out the sides. It was around Christmas (lest the drama not be heightened enough) and I really wanted to go to Jean and Steve Smith's annual Christmas party. About four o'clock I got too discouraged; I figured I should have started dressing yesterday to be ready in time what with two things and another. I called Jean and told her I couldn't possibly figure out how to get myself together without causing people to retch. She said, "Kid, I'll make you a bet very few people notice. Most people at a big party are really worried about how *they* look. Come on . . . You'll have fun. Believe me."

The brilliant analyst and adviser I had finally found gave me her oversized black Porsche sunglasses. (A footnote or headnote: I would never call my analyst a shrink, she is doing just the opposite. She is expanding my head. Can I call her my "expand"?) I put on the tape, the glasses, hot pink lipstick and jacket to match, and Jean was right. People told me how well I looked the way they always did, a social speech tic after a certain age in a certain society.

I got over that party, but others were coming up—not to mention the big one, our twenty-fifth wedding anniversary.

I knew that there were four old gray file cabinets in one of the closets. It was hard to get at them, because there were so many homeless objects piled in front and on top of them: small, crumpled pieces of wrapping paper, used boxes that had been saved for next Christmas for ten years, fabric remnants from skirts, dresses, couches, curtains, costumes that had long since passed on to that big middle-class house in the sky, a white hooked rug that the dog had peed on, and countless empty shopping bags, unfolded, just standing there like out-of-work invaders from the planet Bloomingdale's.

I wanted to get at those files, because I knew that they contained memorabilia connected to our wedding. I was surprised at how careful a record we had kept. There were many folders marked WEDDING.

I put them all out on the bed. The newspaper clippings were

Dick Avedon's photo of Adolph and me on our wedding day.

Rodman Flender took this later one after our twenty-fifth-anniversary party.

yellowed and brittle and some of them crumbled in my hands. Someone had subscribed to a clipping service, so, besides the usual announcements and column items that appeared in the then many New York papers, there were hundreds of copies of small news releases—ADOLPH GREEN TO MARRY ACTRESS—from towns all over the country.

I found telegrams of congratulations from forgotten names and some surprising famous dead people. There was a floor plan of the ballroom of the Sheraton East, which had once been called the Ambassador. It was on Park Avenue in the Fifties and was very elegant. Now it's called . . . Gone, and I'm sorry about that.

The thrill was to find all the pictures. We had hired the regulation photographers, but as a surprise, our friend Dick Avedon had brought along a little no-flash camera, and what a difference. The civilian photos show a bunch of nice people looking somewhat stilted and uncomfortable at a wedding. Dick's pictures look like a fantasy ball full of beautiful spirits. And that's how it was . . . how it felt to me. I looked so pretty and fresh and happy in the pictures. I got an idea.

I rushed into the next room to the really demented cedar storage, loser-of-people closet. It's very deep with two hanging racks on either side, and shelves that go up to the very high ceiling. It is stuffed with old gowns, kids' clothes, overcoats, capes, lamp bases, posters, and coffee urns. The top shelves hold stacks of my old musical arrangements. (How much am I bid for an unused twenty-page chart for a big band of "Oh I Can't Sit Down," from *Porgy and Bess* that has never been used on the Johnny Carson show for which it was intended?) The other shelves have scrapbooks, boxes marked MERRY WIDOWS, BRAS AND GIRDLES; OLD SUMMER T-SHIRTS; and, oh God, WEDDING GOWN.

That's what I'd come for. As I tried to get it down, a hanger fell and almost blinded me, two smaller unseen boxes fell and hit me on the head. But, never mind, there it was . . . just like in the photographs . . . almost. The satin gown, which was called eggshell in those days at Saks Fifth Avenue's Bridal, was now more in the egg yolk family. There were deeper yellow perspiration stains under the arms, even though I had sent it to a million-dollar cleaner before I put it away, but it was still pretty. I tried it on, because my plan, my idea, was maybe to wear it to our anniversary party, for fun. For poignancy. To save money on a new dress. To be theatrical.

It wasn't the cliché of how tight it was, like a scene from "Father Knows Best," although it was a bit difficult to zip up all the way. It did go up to the waist, and then it was a struggle. I left it like that. I put on the wedding hat, a big floppy white organdy rose that sat straight over my bangs with a hair clip. I didn't have the veil anymore. Now, I really looked O.K. for twenty-five years later, by any standards, except for the visible reminders of the recent unpleasantness. Of course my bosom hasn't grown back yet and I decided not to wear the getup. I didn't much feel like going to the party . . . and besides, I looked like Miss Havisham in *Great Expectations*.

After that I started hallucinating silver . . . silver . . . And I got completely carried away. I so wanted to be a walking illustration of aging gracefully (if at all) . . .

"Brave little tyke (after what she's been through) . . ."

"God she looks a knockout . . ."

"Why, she would be great for my new musical . . . *Hi Yo, Silver, A Woman's View of the Lone Ranger*."

What I had done was sabotage a good designer by getting a silver and black collage top over a silver long wraparound skirt that showed my legs when I sat. I tried it on and I looked like a combination of O. J. Simpson and Marlene Dietrich. Disaster. The party is now five minutes and many blocks away. We're the guests of honor. Adolph is pacing, and I'm still in my bathroom. I put on an old reliable white lace dress that was about to fall apart. We were on time, I looked swell, and the party was memorable.

Well, "Life goes on," as Oscar Wilde once said. Trips came and went. Dressing for a ninety-five degree day in Dublin, when my suitcase was full of sensible flannel and wool garments. Getting dressed to meet my son's future mother-in-law in London, same hot weather, same suitcase. . . . She appears . . . long and thin and dark, and coolly throwaway chic—appropriate plissé or piqué. I maintain my gray flannel front and face to match. And then . . . day of days . . . the wedding of my firstborn son. An hour before it was time to get dressed in the youthful, pretty, elegant, yet slightly punk dress it had taken me days of shopping, months of fretting, and hordes of friends to find, I talked to myself. I said, "Phyllis, it is a beautiful day. You simply must not spend it in the bathroom preparing, and crying. It is hardly the end of the world; it is a beginning of something wonderful for him and for you: from this day forth you are a mother-in-law and a grown-up. You will relegate getting dressed to its proper time and priority. You will now go for a walk, maybe see some paintings and then launch into the new secure you and them." I did that. I was Reebokking along Madison Avenue, fresh from the Fairfield Porter show, mulling the inevitabilities and pace of life (always a serious mistake), when . . . whoa . . . twist . . . hurdle . . . outstretched   arms . . . thud . . . pavement . . . "Yes, please, could you just put me into a taxi . . . No, I'm O.K. . . . ow! . . . ow! Doctor . . . no time . . . just bandage it temporarily . . . son . . . wedding . . . about to start."

Dazed, back in my bathroom . . . how to get dressed, over above under and through a fractured ankle???? No panty hose . . . no hose . . . One black sock . . . two black sneakers . . . one old skirt . . . one old big pink jacket . . . one new cane. . . . No mascara please, I'm driving. . . . half a pain-killer.

I made it. They made it.

What have I learned? I have learned to get dressed in the face, neck, head, shoulders, and feet of physical adversity. I have learned that getting dressed is only half the fun . . . the real fun is fantasizing how you're going to look when you finally get it all together, when your body sings, when you find the perfect pale peach blouse for the gray silk something, when your closet is in order and your shoes match anything . . . and your skin clears up and changes texture . . . and you are filled with serene self-confidence. And maybe . . . just maybe . . . when we all meet in that great dressing room in the sky, we'll find out that we were paid by the hour.

ELEVEN

I want to tell you about right after a . . . about two nights after the first operation, while I was waiting to hear if the cancer had spread, whether the fabled lymph nodes had been affected. How many? What the hell was the story? Adolph and I were in my hospital room alone. One of my assigned doctors, a general practitioner, came in to see me.

He said, "Well, you must be very happy. No nodes were involved." (These are phrases that become so alarmingly common that their repetition coming from your own mouth or going into your own ears repels you on every possible level, except when it is good news.)

"What do you mean? How do you know?"

"Oh, I thought you had been told. I just saw it on the computer. Your surgeon will tell you officially. But that's good, good news."

"Are you sure . . . it's not a mistake?"

"No. I saw it. Relax, sleep well. You're very lucky."

"Oh my God . . . " And then the tears, the release came. For both of us. We couldn't hug each other vigorously, physically, but our hands and his lips could.

"I am lucky . . . God hasn't passed me by. I feel like the old . . . oh, thank you, thank you."

We got right on the phone. We called my sisters Shirley and Elaine and my friends Cynthia and Bobbie, but not the children because we didn't want them to be aware of the turbulent details on a day-to-day basis, although we had told them everything up to then. The whole was difficult enough for them to deal with, we thought. We clucked, we congratulated ourselves, we spoke and thought endless variations of "The worst is over" theme. After Adolph left for the night, I told my nurse. She took it in her nurse stride, but nothing could press down my rising feelings.

The next morning my surgeon came in for his rounds. He had my favorite saintly Nurse Donahue with him. They checked the bandage, the sutures, and a slight infection that had developed. I babbled on and on about my great luck. Now, it's not that any look passed from one to another. It's not like their faces moved, it's that somehow no one was cracking a bottle of champagne over my head in celebration.

I got very silent. My turn was over.

The doctor said: "It's absolutely true. There is no node involvement, but this type of . . . malignancy is a fairly invasive one. So it is our recommendation . . . and I've talked this over with my associates and shown all the reports and the tissue sample to our oncologist (new word for me then . . . now part of the vocabulary, like in "God bless Mommy, Daddy, and my nice oncologist"), and we agree that some additional therapy would be advisable."

Scratch my newfound confidence. Scratch a reasonably uncontorted face. Replace with a crumpled, terror-struck, old child.

"What kind of therapy?"

"Well, that's up to the oncologist, he will decide the most effective . . . substances."

I get the words out, but not easily, kid, not easily at all.

"Do you mean chemotherapy? . . . I have to have chemotherapy? Is that what you're saying?"

Now Nurse Donahue, gently, reasonably, and firmly tells me I have an option not to do it but they strongly recommend it. She's wonderful, but they both want to get out of there. So do I.

I'm given the names of three oncologists connected with the hospital. They each have a different plan, as this is all still fairly experimental. The first one, who was the choice of the surgeon, is fortyish young, with a thick head of prematurely gray hair and a mustache to match. He is slim, tall, and good-looking. He gets my vote before he opens his mouth, and it's a good thing. Because he doesn't open it much and only for very short periods of time. He makes Gary Cooper seem like Joan Rivers (well, not really). He is taciturn, soft-voiced, cool-eyed, demisyllabic. He doesn't want to get involved, one figures. You can't blame him, one rationalizes. But you want to shake him, physically and metaphorically, until he says, "Gee, I'm sorry."

His plan is for me to start right away. As a matter of fact he says he has the best results when he starts it right after the operation. Then I would come in once a week to take three drugs intravenously and two by mouth every day for six months. Never mind what they do. The idea is, lower but more frequent doses which should, *should* produce fewer side effects.

Now we all know the first question everyone asks. We all know that a bald head is the terrifying symbol of cancer to too many people. When I asked, he said, "Well, there's no guarantee, but we've had very good results with this method . . . and I would think you'll be O.K."

Can you imagine? Someone in the medical profession actually saying that? And I believed him. Somehow I believed him. I guess that when people who don't say much *do* say something it counts for more. Don't write to me about how obvious that is.

The second oncologist was very sympathetic, understanding, and slightly older. He had a somewhat different timetable and drug combination. He said since my hair was thin, it was possible I would lose it. And then he said, "It's not your hair I would worry about . . . it's your other breast."

Somewhere in all the information that had been fed into Adolph and me, I vaguely—can you imagine, but it's true—I *vaguely* remembered one sentence, *one sentence* about . . . biopsy other breast . . . some unusual cell formations. I shut it out again. Too much. Too soon. Too late. Forget it. The important thing to me at that moment was that this doctor was treating a well-known, talented actress I knew. And she was touring. He had arranged for her to have her treatments in various other cities. That was promising. I gave him a slight advantage.

I never got to the third candidate's office. When I called for an appointment the nurse or secretary asked me humiliating questions in an antagonistic manner over the phone. I judged him by her—although he had an outside private office which meant I wouldn't have to keep going back to that hospital and sit for hours surrounded by heartbreaking reminders of the corporal minority I was now part of.

Adolph and I mulled and chewed, but not for long. I think we all knew that the original doctor's plan seemed right. I went out to the country for a few days to walk on the beach and drink cold martinis at night, which was Nurse Donahue's prescription. And then I came back. Not refreshed and not ready—never ready—to start. This was sometime in late June. I had a benefit performance for Guild Hall in East Hampton scheduled for mid-July. I was to do a solo concert. I've seen too many MGM movies. I decided to try to do it. . . .

There was no way I could do it alone so I asked Adolph and Betty, and the wonderful composer Cy Coleman, if they would do most of the evening, then I could do just a few songs. They all agreed, and I started rehearsing and planning. Of course it made me feel better to have my mind on other things. Somehow I got through it. It wasn't fun, it wasn't satisfying, I wasn't very good. I wasn't ready yet. I was just trying to be a "courageous and adorable human being." I wasn't fair to myself. The performance was over. They all performed brilliantly and were wonderful and generous. I felt even more depressed and lost. Someone kindly offered her house and gave a reception for us afterward, but I didn't go, I sent Adolph and the kids. I said I was too tired and exhausted. I guess I wanted to make sure that they all knew what a trouper I had been, and how delicate I really was.

The truth was that I felt fine physically, and had lots of energy, but I was angry with everyone because I had cancer and they didn't. I walked around our house that we had rebuilt three years after the fire, and yelled and cried and convinced myself they were all shits, otherwise why would I be alone after the enormous sacrifice I had just made. You know what I thought? I thought that if I ever had a "fatal disease" or something terrible happened to me the world would change. Not me. The world. People would automatically love me, pay attention to me, hire me, invite me, give me presents, never get angry with me, admire me. That I would become beautiful and thin and that every other aspect of my life would right itself in order to balance this lopsided blow to me.

When Adolph got home I let him have it in an irrational and mean-spirited way. The children heard me in their rooms, and it must have both frightened them and alienated them from their "newly sick" mother.

I was constantly evaluating my family and my friends: How are they treating me now? How are they responding? How are they supporting me? I didn't want my children to be the ones who had a mother who had cancer, but I simply couldn't read how they were dealing with it. Or I didn't want to. It never occurred to me that they were as frightened and angry as I was and they didn't know what to do. I didn't realize then that I had a cocoon of Adolph and Cynthia and Bobbie. They were my costars in this drama, and the kids were put in supporting-player roles.

"Bobbie" is Barbara Handman, whom I met in the late fifties when I started studying acting with her husband, Wynn.

Many of Wynn's young acting students hung out at their small apartment, and took turns baby-sitting with the Handmans' beautiful and precocious daughter, Laura Rose. Even then, when she was in her mid-twenties, Bobbie was serene, mature, wise, and motherly to all of us, though we were not that much younger than she. Their family became ours. It was a nurturing atmosphere. I always felt welcome, wanted, better, when I was with her.

Many of us in the acting class remained friends, but our link was and is Bobbie, who made each one of us feel that we were not only able, but duty-bound, to expand our intellectual, artistic, and political universes. Bobbie pays attention to you, she listens to you, her internal spending of time seems to belong to another culture.

She had her second child, Liza, around the same time I had Amanda, and Betty Bacall had her third child, Sam Robards. Our kids grew up together. Liza and Amanda went through lower school together, roomed together at college, and have remained extremely close friends. My son Adam was best man at Sam's wedding. They all seem to be there for each other. Am I hitting you over the head friendship-wise? Probably. But, as you might have gleaned by now, I take these gifts ever so seriously.

I was constantly complaining about the kids to Adolph. They hadn't come to the hospital enough. I couldn't count on them. But when Amanda had come, there was almost always someone there. I still don't know what to do in hospital rooms, why should she? She'd bring me something and I'd make much too much of a fuss about it. I would either be tearfully jolly or nervous about how she was acting or about her discomfort. How wonderful it would have been if I could have been authentic. What's authentic?

I'm ashamed to tell you that I behaved really badly to my family and friends for a long time. Strangers, coworkers, other women waiting with me for the "treatments," the receptionist at the hospital, the doctor, the nurses who put the needle in my vein on the back of my hand through which those mysterious drugs flowed—the audiences—saw a together, joking, take-charge, brave, always laughing lady.

A couple of months into my treatments I was offered two jobs. With the arrogance of terror I took them both. One was to play the wife in Clifford Odets's play *Rocket to the Moon* at the Hartman Theatre in Stamford, Connecticut, with a wonderful director, Ed Sherin, and a cast that included Lou Jacobi and Tony Franciosa. "Yes! Certainly . . . you bet." Then I was asked by a lively, very young group of comedians to direct a revue of theirs in a cabaret in New York. "Yes . . . why not? . . . great!" Oh, they would overlap at some point. Well, I'll work it out. And the treatments . . . Well, the doc said to keep busy, that work was the answer, the more time I had to think the worse I'd feel. There were women waiting with me for their chemotherapy who had nine-to-five jobs every day and kept them.

I told both managements about the other job, and I assured them that there would be no conflicts. I didn't know what I was talking about.

The revue started first, and for the first week or so I enjoyed it, although I never developed what's called rapport with the group. They were talented and I wanted to do right by them, but they all had worked together many times before, and had written their own material. They were used to being directed by one of their own.

I didn't want to face too much. I was working, I was moving fast. Maybe reality wouldn't catch me. Then the rehearsals for the play started days, while the revue was previewing nights. Once a week I was getting the "stuff" at the hospital. (Note: Important. If you ever have to take a regimen of drugs, memorize the names, and each time you're to get them, ask: "I'm getting A, B, and C, right?" Sometimes there are what's called mix-ups. As they say on television every three seconds: take responsibility.)

I thought I was doing a brilliant balancing act. I had also accepted a high-paying singing concert—in the Midwest—which I had to cancel because I had no time to rehearse that, too. Then the cabaret people fired me a few days before the opening. They had gotten another director. They would give me full credit, but I was out.

They were right. I had done what I thought was a good job, up to a point—the point where I had to start concentrating on the Odets play, on my acting, and learning and developing the role. Rehearsals for the play were held in a dimly lit meeting room of a church on the Upper West Side. The surroundings depressed the hell out of me, especially on Wednesdays, when I went there straight from my chemotherapy treatment. I felt an unsettling, unspecific queasiness. I had a slightly sour, very metallic taste in my mouth. I drank endless Coca-Colas and sucked on endless hard candies. It was never terrible, but you know how you can't remember pain? I can't, but I can summon the taste, and the feeling of the chemicals invading my whole being. Nothing really took the taste away then or takes it away now from my memory.

When I was fired from the revue, I was stung and angry. The new director changed everything I had done, including sets, costumes, and the running order. My name remained on the program and in ads and press releases. I asked the press agent to inform the critics that I was really not the director anymore.

Well, *The New York Times* gave the show an excellent review and noted what I had requested. They said it really didn't matter who was responsible. It was an ethical but dumb move. I was trying to display my workable health to the theatrical community and instead they all read that I had been replaced.

Now I could concentrate on playing the unattractive, unwanted, rather tiresome Odets character. I really got into it; I let her take me over—self-pity was the name of the game on- and offstage. I felt none of the energetic joy that had sustained me since I was a child, during rehearsals and performances.

The play opened in Connecticut—to varied response. I wore a cheap thirties-style wig, because I was still afraid that my hair would fall out. I wouldn't let anyone come near me in the dressing room to help me in and out of my clothes. During the hour's drive to and from the theater I would listen to my Walkman. I didn't chat it up with Tony, Lou, and Bruce, my car mates. I didn't tell anyone what was going on. I wanted them to know instinctively and to feel sorry for me, admire me, and save me. I was at war with myself and everybody else.

I would complain bitterly to my friends Cynthia and Bobbie on the phone, late at night. Their voices and intelligence and concern suffused, comforted, and stimulated me. They wondered why I would put myself through all this, and what I was trying to prove and to whom.

I had no answers that were consistent with any philosophical or medical beliefs, except the famous old Bessarabian dictum, "Get out of the house."

As I said, none of the dread physical things were happening. I hadn't gained the threatened weight from the cortisone drug Prednisone, my hair was intact, but when I looked in the mirror every night while I was getting made up, I saw a woman I didn't much like or feel close to. It was a terrible time to disapprove of myself, but the truth is, I didn't turn out the way I thought I would.

All my genuine faith, spirituality, and optimism had taken a sabbatical. Cynthia could not understand why I was not working with the nutritionist I had seen and listened to all the time when I was healthy. I knew he had helped many cancer and chemo-therapy patients with a regimen of vitamin and mineral supple-ments to bolster the attacked immune system. She and I had both clucked and been furious with Felicia for pooh-poohing any nontraditional aids during her illness, and here was I . . . you get it.

Here's the difference. I eventually let myself "be persuaded" to get his help. I took many mouthfuls of supplements daily, and started to feel more energetic, my color improved, and some-times—just sometimes—my mood registered normal instead of moribund or hysterical.

During some of this time, Adolph was in Budapest, acting in a film, *Lily in Love*, with Maggie Smith and Christopher Plum-mer. When he had been offered the part and the opportunity to spend time in his ancestral country, he had wanted to turn it down. He thought it was too difficult a time to leave me alone. I urged him to do it. I was and am very proud of his having an unsolicited movie acting career at this time of his life. He spoke Hungarian before he spoke English, so there was some kind of poetic justice at work here. He and Betty rarely worked alone so he had made it a condition of his contract that they pay her air fare there and put her up at a hotel so that the two of them could continue writing. He had also done that when he had made the movie *My Favorite Year*, only it was a shorter distance to Los Angeles. My doctor had told me that it would be possible to miss a treatment and make it up at the end, so that I could visit Adolph when the run of my play was over. He had been casual about it, so I felt assured that it would not impede my recovery.

People kept marveling at my ability to work, to travel, to be so cheerful. I accepted their compliments. I chose not to reveal to anyone, including myself at times, that my fuel was rage, unbridled, all-consuming rage. I guess if you got all the angry people together in one choleric plant, there'd never be a power shortage anywhere in the world.

I had also resisted—no, rejected—any of the postsurgery or ongoing support programs offered by the hospital and affiliated groups. The thought of "sharing" these events with a roomful, or even a couchful, of women seemed mindless and beneath me. I was wrong, almost dead wrong. Now I know what I really feared was that if I heard their stories, or felt myself to be part of any minority community, I would lose my feeling of experiencing a unique tragedy. Today I would urge anyone to avail herself of the thoughtful and loving groups and advisers that are everywhere.

Right after the operation, a couple of the doctors had advised me to have a visit or two with a psychiatrist at the hospital who specialized in the emotional problems of women with breast cancer. She was well known and very respected in certain circles that I wish I'd never gotten into.

"Not for me . . . not necessary, thank you very much" was my terse and contemptuous response then. But a moment, or rather a very long series of moments, of unrelieved hopelessness led me finally to call this doctor and make an appointment. Her nurse asked questions that I thought were too personal, in a detached manner, as if she were a Western Union operator reading back a business telegram.

I said, "I choose to tell all this directly to the doctor, if you don't mind."

"But she needs this information . . . stop . . . before she sees you."

"Well, she'll just have to wing it."

"Please believe me, Mrs. Green . . . this attitude is not useful to you . . . me or the doctor. We work with a lot of women . . . and we've found this to be helpful."

"Thanks, but no thanks. Good-bye."

The setting is an extremely small office in a metropolitan hospital. It's like one big filing cabinet. The desk is gray and steely, the prospective analyst is blond and steely; she is wearing a long white hospital coat.

The patient enters and sits in a metal chair alongside the you know who and what. She starts crying by the second question, which is something penetrating, like: Do you have medical insurance?

The patient tries to spill her guts, the doctor starts discussing the effectiveness of mood-elevating drugs. She is well into the possible side effects of Elavil, dry mouth, lassitude, longitude, before the drippy patient says:

"I don't want to take any more drugs. I want to feel better. I want to learn how to live with it . . . to get better . . . to grow. . . . "

The doctor looks at her with great empathy as she writes out the prescription for Elavil.

Bill: eighty-five dollars.

On the top floor of a brownstone in the Upper West Nineties, a semiretired Freudian, heavily accented, old, old hot shot has made room for this seriously ill actress. She again spills her guts accompanied by heavily mascaraed tears:

ILL ACTRESS: Oh, please . . . can you help me?

DOCTOR: You tell me, I don't know.

ILL ACTRESS: I've written a few pages about how I feel. I've brought them with me. Maybe they would be helpful.

DOCTOR: Good . . . good. We'll talk about it next time. Do you want to make an appointment? My time is very limited.

ILL ACTRESS: Oh, of course, surely, certainly, definitely, anytime, thank you.

DOCTOR (looking in frayed, clothbound book): Thursday at ten?

ILL ACTRESS: Good, great, yes, fine, thank you. *(She hands him her few typewritten pages.)*

DOCTOR: Do you think you are serious and will continue with these sessions?

ILL ACTRESS: *(smelling a Freudian rat):* I don't know.

DOCTOR: I don't really want to bother reading this, if I'm not going to treat you.

ILL ACTRESS: *(taking pages out of his old hand):* Right, I understand, I see, O.K. I'll see you Thursday.

Second session canceled by ill actress.
Bill: two hundred dollars for two sessions.

In the end I swallowed my pride and a teeny fistful of Valium, and went to see the first choice, the real expert with the nurse I'd wanted to kill.

This doctor was kind, sympathetic, intelligent, and a peach of a listener. She read my pages, and was complimentary. She told me it took a lot of time and that I was too hard on myself. She understood my resistance to taking a mood elevator, but she pointed out that I was taking (not all together but at various times) Xanax, Serax, Valium, Darvocet, Percocet, Dalmane, and hot cocoa. She suggested that it might be better to trade all those attempts for one that she felt might help me. I was afraid to. It seemed the final giving-in and giving-up action.

A few weeks later I was in the country, in our house surrounded with my family and close friends on a perfectly beautiful Sunday, and I decided to give the old Elavil a try. Why? Because there seemed no way out or up from the depths and darkness of my despair. Now we are all extremely aware of the power of the mind and how she does funny things. Well, I had an attack of every side effect that I had ever heard about since childhood. I thought I was losing my mind. I was dizzy, I was anxious, I was dry-mouthed, I was tired, I cried, I saw stars, I heard singing, and there was no one there. I panicked and threw out the bottle of pills.

I was now seeing no one and taking nothing but anything I could get my hands on. I got through with the chemotherapy,

finished the treatment, and went for the happy last visit. Charlotte (a friend who had had a mastectomy and chemotherapy)
went with me and in her fearless way asked the question both
Adolph and I had never addressed, let alone mailed.

"What about the other breast?"

Now I don't want to quote the doctor falsely, but the gist was
he told Charlotte that he was not remotely worried.

> CHARLOTTE: Did you hear that?
> ME: Yes.
> CHARLOTTE: Did you really hear that?
> ME: Yes, but how can he be so sure? Do you mean it all just went
> away?
> CHARLOTTE: Either that or he just doesn't know what the fuck he's
> talking about.

That night I met Adolph and Gloria Jones for dinner. Adolph
told me that I had had a call from the doctor and that I should
call him tomorrow. He said it was nothing to worry about.

> GLORIA: Oh, shit, what a thing to think about.
> ADOLPH: I shouldn't have told you.
> ME: You sure shouldn't have.
> ADOLPH: He said nothing to worry about. He would have told me
> if there was anything.
> ME: Then why did he call?

I'll tell you why he called. After I left, he must have actually
read the *War and Peace*–size medical data I had amassed.

He sent me to another round of surgeons to get their opinions.

The first, some butcher on the East Side with Adolf Eich-
mann's charm, said, "You're sitting on a time bomb, little lady."
He had the most crowded office of all. Don't anyone tell me that
women aren't masochists.

The second, an internist to the stars, sat opposite me and
looked at that same medical information. With the turn of each

page, his face got graver and lumpier, involuntary Ohs escaped from his thin lips.

The last doctor I saw was Charlotte's. I liked him. He said he would read my medical records that night and call me the next day in the country. When he called and told me what I already knew, it seemed like my last bit of oxygen had been taken away. Another spring, another life test.

I was really afraid and ashamed to tell you this. I thought you might say, "Who is she kidding? She must be rich . . . she's sort of famous . . . why should she be crying those particular blues?" But sometime between one and two, my goddamned health insurance ran out. The Catch-22 of show business health plans. I had been earning and paying for thirty years. But the rules of the AFTRA (American Federation of TV and Radio Artists) union were then that if you didn't earn one thousand dollars in a given year under their jurisdiction . . . your insurance was canceled. Well, I sure as hell wasn't pursuing work in TV away from New York where my doctors and chemotherapy treatments were, so just when I needed it most (because as you well know medical costs are structured to insurance plans, not people's plans) it ran out and I wasn't covered adequately anywhere.

I had to get some television work quickly so that at least I could get coverage for the next period. I felt like a Theodore Dreiser character. I had earned so much money from television at various times, and now I couldn't figure out how to earn a thousand dollars.

I also had to face something I hadn't until then. Would people not hire me because they would be afraid that I'd die on them? I had neither hidden nor publicized what had happened. My only focus was living.

I would have begged, but I didn't have the guts. I let other people do it for me. I told my friend Ruth Berle. She called Freddy de Cordova, producer of the Johnny Carson show, and told him my problem.

"Are you kidding? We love her, Johnny loves her . . . it's no favor. She's on next week. We'll fly her out!"

Neither he nor Johnny ever mentioned it . . . nor have I until now. I want them to know how important it was.

I asked Adolph to call Mark Goodson, my beloved boss of my many years on TV game shows. Same immediate response. I had my coverage.

I know I've written very little about my children. I respect their privacy. They are, without question, the source of my greatest and deepest pleasure. They're very different from each other. Yet they share abundant gifts, strength of character, and my love and continual interest.

As I was trying to absorb the fact that I needed a second operation, Adolph, Amanda, and I were beginning to rehearse for a play called *The New Yorkers*. It was the first time we had ever acted together. The Trinity School, where Amanda had been a student, was opening a new theater. The first production was to be two new one-act plays by the gifted writer Murray Schisgal. The people at the school thought that it would be attention-getting to have an alumna and her fairly well-known theatrical parents in it. They were right.

Both Adolph and I thought that it would be a wonderful opportunity for Amanda. She was finishing her junior year at Brown, studying theater among other things, acting in a variety of plays, and doing all the backbreaking work associated with college theater. She is an unusually talented actress and performer, and you all know about the wildly mixed blessing of being the child of parents who are established in the field you're pursuing. (See *Mommie Dearest,* Liza Minnelli, and whoever Meryl Streep Junior is.)

In the first play, which was about two immigrants, Amanda would act opposite her father, and in the second, about an upwardly mobile couple celebrating their anniversary, Adolph and I would play ourselves as seen through Schisgal's comic mind.

We were about two weeks into rehearsal when I decided to go in and get the second operation over with. I stayed with the same surgeon because I did and do have complete confidence in him. We promised Trinity that we would do the plays in the fall.

TWELVE

My husband, Bobbie, and Charlotte had come with me when I checked into the hospital. They held my bags and talked to a starchy administrative lady, while in the admitting suite the nurses took my blood and measured my heartbeats. . . . Oh, that was a good one. . . . You know when they take your EKG, they put suction cups around your heart? Well, picture this: I mean you had to be there. There was this problem . . . with my *flat* side and the cups kept falling off.

But do you want to know the hardest part of being admitted? It's giving all your insurance numbers and data. You sit there in a little office with a perfectly nice, heavily accented person, and pretend that this is just some normal red tape, like getting a driver's license, or having your cat fixed, when she knows, as you know, that this is the admission to heartbreak house. I was, I would dare say, at my most civilized and charming. A few conspiratorial pleasantries about how complicated they make it for you. A polite inquiry into the country of origin of Ms. Blue Cross. No, I don't remember where she was from, because I was fooling . . . I was playing a part . . . I was scared out of my mind, into my mind, and through my mind.

You are always admitted the day before the actual operation, so it was quite early when I arrived at my room. It was private and spare with one picture hanging on the wall opposite the hospital bed. It was a reproduction of a copy of an unknown artist's rendering of a vase of flowers on a black background. There were a couple of plastic chairs, a nightstand, a chest of drawers, and that long Formica top on chrome legs and wheels that fits over the top of the bed. The private bath was complete with a handrail next to the toilet, and by the sink, complimentary surgical soap, mouthwash, Handi-Wipes and voilà, mesdames and messieurs! This will be your home for the next week or so, or however long it takes you to recover, or cool . . . as the case may be.

My two friends, my husband and I do busywork. We all start unpacking with demonic energy—nightgowns, panties in drawers, vodka on top of drawers to add a festive air. I paste my crumpled piece of legal-size, yellow-lined paper over the painting. You see, the last time, I wrote my reasons for getting and staying well on this paper. I meant them then . . . I sort of mean them now. I'll tell you what they are later when we get to the inspirational part. Don't worry. That won't be for a long time.

So now we're all unpacked and hanging around with nothing to do in this here hospital room. We all sort of half-circle the bed. Everyone thinking but no one saying that tomorrow at this time I'll be lying there, sedated, an operatee, a patient, at the mercy of . . . dependent upon . . . terrified by . . . uncomfortable with . . . and powerless to.

We take a drink, we laugh a lot, we make a fuss about going for more crushed ice and paper cups. A call comes, there is a package downstairs. Charlotte goes to get it. She brings back smoked salmon, black bread, lemons. It is a feast. We start to mellow in a hysterical way. We all flop on the bed now, eating and drinking and toasting Charlotte for her generosity.

Once again for a short while, the room was a beehive, a mare's nest. Sometimes it looked like the stateroom scene from the Marx Brothers movie *A Night at the Opera*. Do you remember that? If you don't, you should see it again, it's good for what ails us.

In the middle of this, two callow, sallow, young, but middle-aged-looking interns came in. They were both dark, with thinning hair; they were both tall, not fat, but bulky. They were both their own fathers already. They were charmless with a fake casual manner that didn't remotely hide their uneasiness at playing doctor. I was crazy about them; I called them Frick and Frack. They were crazy about me, especially when I looked at them with vodka-soaked steely eyes and told them—in response to their request to examine my breast—"Not on your fucking life. By tomorrow it won't be there, so what the hell do I care what you find? You need practice? Go to the charity wards and feel up some poor bugger who doesn't understand English. I'll be damned if your fingers are the last touch I feel on my soon to be late booby!"

They told me they had to give me an internal exam.

"Are you crazy? . . . Have you lost your assorted marbles? . . . Poke up and in me? . . . Dummies . . . I wouldn't even let you toss a salad for me . . . bug off . . . get out . . . give your parents back the med school money . . . get an honest job . . . you have no gift . . . Frick and Frack, fuck you!"

Meanwhile Charlotte decided to spread some sunshine in the next room, where a nice lady on her next to last day in the hospital was nicely recovering from a you know what. My husband told me later that Charlotte dragged him in, too, as she said: "Well, don't you look lovely, dear? Are you feeling all right? You know, my good friend is next door. She's having her second, you know; it's fairly elective at the moment. . . . I had mine done almost three years ago, and the reconstruction a year later, and it is really swell. Do you want to see it?" Without waiting for an answer from this dumbstruck stranger, she shooed my husband out, and, in a flash, whipped her smocklike shirt up, covering her face, uncovering her two—yes, they are really swell—breasts. "I bet you can't tell which twin has the Toni, can you? Well, actually, if you put your mind on the case you can. I mean it's not exactly foolproof . . . Well, I've got to go. Good luck to you, dear. If you ever need anything call me. I'm always

home. I'll give you the name of my plastic man. . . . I hope I
didn't disturb you. I'm drunk, don't you know? I hate being in a
hospital again. It's hard. I want to help my friend, but I gave at
the office. Bye."

Betty Bacall is a star, a real star. She's big, as in tall and statu-
esque. She has big, strong beauty, bones, hair, extravagant gestures and laugh, and a forceful, intimidating manner. Everyone
in the hospital wanted to get a look at her.

She came in a little later on that first day, just as the food and
mood were wearing thin. She came with great sandwiches and
cakes, and by that time Cynthia and my daughter Amanda had
arrived. We started eating and drinking and laughing too loud
again. We were bursting out of the room. Betty B. got them to
bring in more chairs. My head was swimming, no, wading in
very murky waters.

I was not able to get drunk; I was not able to put aside the
realization that soon they would all be able to go home, slightly
woozy, thanking God that it wasn't them left in this room. My
husband was getting more and more pissed and vague. Why
not? The last time, he stayed with me all night before the operation. He slept on a cot, the way I slept with my son when he was
a baby and having a hernia operation. And with my baby girl
when she had a hospital "procedure." This time it seemed super-
fluous; after all I was a vet. I'd been through it. Anyway, it's just
ever so slightly embarrassing and pathetic the second time. The
vigor and sense of adventure are gone. I mean that. It's like the
second wedding. Or the night after the opening of a mildly
successful show. You've given it your best shot, now it's yesterday's bad news.

Well, the moment of truth, as they say, finally arrived. The
nurse had come and given me the rundown on tomorrow. I was
to be the first operation of the day. That's good. Don't forget
that! You get it over with. The surgeon is fresh, nurses are crisp,
needles are clean, birds are singing . . . and you know what? I'd
gotten to be such a hospital creep that I was actually happy about
it.

I was left with a spiffy hospital gown, not in a high color like on TV, but a faded white, skimpy, snaps missing, strings chewed, totally humiliating article of nonclothing. During this, my gang was out of the room, probably hanging out in the lounge. When they all came back, the atmosphere changed significantly. I found myself lying on the bed, the victim sensation spreading through me. I couldn't even manage to call the nurse an asshole. If Frick and Frack had come in, I would have let them play "Yankee Doodle" on my ribs. There were no assholes anymore, anywhere in the world, except me.

One by two by three, my visitors left until there was just Adolph and me. The alcohol had worn off, and there was little to say. We reviewed the day, the jokes, the food, the frustrations. He dug down into his deepest being, pulled up every muscle, summoned up breath he hadn't used in years, and seemed to grow taller. He self-inflated in order to say: "Honey, I know you're going to be all right, really . . . really. This is awful . . . awful, but you're going to pull through this like the champ you've always been and come out the other side. We both will. It's been a shitty year, but you made the right choice. You . . . *We'll* be stronger than ever. We have each other. We have our wonderful children. Everybody loves you. Everybody. . . . There's never been anyone as loved as you are. You know that's true. . . . You've never looked more beautiful. . . . My darling . . . my wife . . . my girl . . . I love you so much . . . I do . . . my baby."

And then I let him go home.

The quiet . . . The quiet then . . . And those hospital sounds over the Dante's *Inferno* PA system: "All available assistance is needed in room ten fourteen. Repeat. Assistance immediately in ten fourteen." Well, you just knew that some poor soul was close to cashing it all in. I put on the TV. It was the size of three boxes of Grape Nuts on an ingenious pulley kind of thing, so you could pulley it right up to your nose from any position on the bed. That's what I did. I smelled all thirteen channels. Nothing. Then I tried reading Marcus Aurelius's *Meditations* and Joan Collins's autobiography. They were equally compelling and inspiring. It all depends on whether you wanted to think or fuck.

The nurse brought in two white pills in a tiny paper cup. They'll give you anything the night before. I started modestly with Ativan, your common anti-anxiety garden variety, and Seconal, your famous "dolls." Nothing. I decided to shower instead of waiting for the morning. I went into the bathroom, held on to all handrails, just for laughs stripped . . . and started howling, terrible sounds made worse because I had to muffle them. I didn't want the nurse to come in. I ripped open the surgical scrub packet—there was a dark gray, thick sponge filled with brown surgical soap, a sort of body Brillo. There was a hand shower in a shower stall, and I scrubbed and screamed . . . and sobbed and scrubbed and . . . Well, you get the picture.

"This is unfair!" From the picture "Why Me, Oh God, Why Me?" And now a musical interlude while the lady tries to sleep and tries more pills, even a smuggled-in suppository from France, guaranteed to dormez vous. . . . How about a few choruses of "Spring Will Be a Little Late This Year"? That's a good song. Think about it and I'll sing it for you. I sing very, very well. It's just what the doctor ordered. That is, just what the patient ordered . . . "La . . . La . . . La . . . La . . . Spring will be . . . a little late this year . . . A little late arriving in my lonely room over here." I don't think those are the right lyrics, but that's what I was singing. I knew the mood. I knew the customers. I've worked this room before.

How do you feel about waking up in the morning, very, very early, not exactly sure of where you are, hearing a voice say (so cheerily you know it's got to be a bad, bad place): *"Ms. You, Ms. You, wake up, Ms. You. . . . We've got a busy day!"*

I'll give you *busy day.* A shot of Demerol. A shot of morphine. A lemon swab on your gums. Nothing by mouth, remember? An attendant comes in to put wheels on your bed, pulling up the metal bar sides so that you can't fall out. A nice long ride in an elevator to the operating room. One killing thing—it was very early, remember, and as I was being rolled out of my room, Bobbie and Cynthia were there smiling, blowing me one good kiss, and telling me they loved me. They did that and I loved that and them. Remember this isn't "Trapper John." This isn't

"St. Elsewhere." This is life, folks, this is real, and they were there and do you have friends like I do? . . . I hope so.

You don't even get the elevator to yourself. It's just a regular run. Other people get on—you smile and try to get that "I'm just a visitor here myself" look on your face. Not too easy. "Just kidding, folks, I can leave anytime I want, you know." Not bloody likely, what with the sedation and straps and all. The drugs just didn't work as well this time. Last time, by this time, is my time, is your time . . . I was gaga city already, fuzzy, and warm all over. This time I was almost all there. I was very aware of the operating room, the nurses, the anesthesiologist, my own surgeon—shiny-faced, pleasant, cool, serious; he was surprised I was so awake. I said, "It's a shitty job, but somebody has to do it!" He didn't laugh a lot. That's the last thing I remember.

THIRTEEN

How does it feel? Very tight across the chest, as though it's huge and bursting. But, of course, there's nothing there but two horizontal scars that don't quite meet at the center and two lumps of excess flesh that come to a point under each arm. Not a pretty sight, I say. Who's seen it? Only the privileged army of doctors and nurses. I'm not Lyndon Johnson, and this isn't glamorous or acceptable surgery, like your appendectomies or your gallstone slice. This was big, bad unmentionable city until the brave and spirited Happy Rockefeller and Betty Ford. I'm not even mentioning it really, if you notice. So let's change the subject.

Let me tell you about the sound my nails make as they tap up and down the full-length mirror that is half of the closet door in our bathroom. The other half is wallpapered in fake Deco gray geometrics that looked good to me ten years ago. Do you know what I mean? . . . I have chosen this mirrored side to do the Reach for Recovery exercises that are illustrated in the perky pink book you are given in the hospital. The illustrations are photographs showing a terrified-looking woman in a black leotard doing the aforementioned and other equally stunning ex-

191

ercises. This particular one has you creeping up the walls with your two arms, letting your fingertips do the walking. The goal? . . . to reach higher and higher. Well, I have these fairly long nails, see? . . . and that sound they make is like a bad Bill Robinson tap routine. Each time going a little higher and a little more frenetically . . . but I have done this before . . . and I never thought I'd have to do this again . . . and it deeply offends my sensibilities, which are many, to do this . . . thing.

I also tried to swim every day to lessen the discomfort and build up those pectorals for possible reconstruction. I couldn't swim in front of anyone for a while. I mean *anyone,* even husband or children, because my bathing costume was too bizarre and I was so embarrassed by my concave chest. I couldn't find a suit that was comfortable or waterproof falsies. I put on a leotard over a big white surgical bra with Kleenex stuffed in the front so it wouldn't rub and irritate the new incision. I threw an oversize T-shirt from some unexotic land over it and started gingerly to move my arms. The crawl was excruciating. The breaststroke . . . don't ask. The backstroke . . . impossible. But I was a hell of a round-shouldered floater. I persevered . . . you bet. For a week it seemed nothing was going to yield without discomfort. I pretended that I was FDR in Warm Springs, Georgia. I shouted "MY FELLOW AMERICANS" to the trees as I dog-paddled.

The next week I was tired of playing hide-and-seek. I went to the pool when my family was there. It was very hard for them to look at me. I know I'm not a paraplegic, I'm not Marlon Brando in *The Men.* But it still ain't easy. It's all relative, my dear, all relative.

I would fix, Walter Mitty–like, on various well-known powerful women and try to imagine how they would handle it. Someone gave me the memoirs of Diana Vreeland, which had just come out. She was so original, so colorful, so manicured red nail on the pulse of fashion. "A godsend, Cookie. Breasts are out. *O-U-T . . . OUT.* They just don't sing with serious clothes. They pull the glorious cloth all out of shape. Best thing that came down you private pike, Bambina. Make it work for you . . . have some new shoes made . . . leave me alone."

I decided that Renata Adler would write a dense novel about its legal aspects and get great reviews. Twyla Tharp would get a grant for the first medical jazz ballet done to Fats Waller's music. Shirley MacLaine would have performed her own surgery because she had been a doctor in a previous life. Joan Didion would have had a nervous breakdown in Central America, and Lillian Hellman would have been really pissed off.

So was I. My body recovered quickly . . . and luckily this time I needed no further powerful chemical therapy. I just continued to take one no-side-effect drug by mouth every day.

It was hard to convince people that I was really all right. When they heard that I'd had another operation, somehow they started writing me off. . . . I could sense it.

What would you like to know about people's responses and attitudes? Do you want to know about their eyes and the game I play?

The ones who haven't seen you since the recent unpleasantness look you in the eyes so straight, and so hard, that your eyes burn and hurt from their reflected intensity. They talk of this and that and these and those, and I never take my eyes off their eyes either. And then I count the seconds before their eyes dart down to my chest to see just what is going on there. Men are slower on the eye take. Women don't wait very long at all to check it out. Well, really, why should they? They're worried about their own, for Christ's sake. They are trying to imagine the feeling. They're anxious to see how you've dressed them. They take it personally, and well they might.

Some of the men are shy about embracing you. I find I do this odd maneuver. I let them hug me, but I never stretch out my arms or share in the embrace. I bend my arms at the elbows and place them directly on my chest, each arm in front of its corresponding falsie. So . . . the guys get two bony arms against their chest instead of rubbery mounds. What a drag . . . for both of us.

Once again I tried to put my career back into working order. Adolph, Amanda, and I honored our commitment to the Trinity School, and went back into rehearsals and opened the theater in the Schisgal play *The New Yorkers*. It was a disaster. Each of us thought we were doing it for the other. The critics were vicious as hell to some of us. I wore a wig again, even though I had no reason to. I did little but worry about Adolph and Amanda though they didn't ask me to. It was a wrong move for me, but nobody put a gun to my head. I was a dope. I remember little about being onstage. . . . Again I was working too soon, and for the wrong reasons.

Soon after the show closed and I had burned all the reviews and certain critics in effigy, I started going down to the loft in SoHo that Cynthia and I shared and used as a studio. I was trying to write a new nightclub act for myself, but I found myself back at the old daydreaming fruit stand. Our room was on the third floor of a walk-up in a small, very old, corner red-brick building, and I spent most of my time looking out the window at that corner. Women and men, no, girls and boys, mostly, walked by with wide hair and shoulders, tapered bottoms and boots. Diagonally across the street was another red monument to a better time, with dark green trim and arches and terra-cotta rosettes, and a six-story crimson fire escape just waiting for a dance from *West Side Story*. There was white sun and black shadows and nothing in between, but those young people pairing, singling, preening, coming out of the dark green health-food restaurant at the street level of that corner which I couldn't take my eyes off when I should have been working, when I wanted to be in the old bar on the other corner.

Talk yourself out of this one, kiddo. What could be the worst thing that could happen? He asks me to come to his studio, or he asks to come to mine, and when we get to one of them I say . . . like Jill Clayburgh might:

"Look, there's something I think you should know . . . " But before I have a chance, he covers my mouth with delicate dry kisses and says gently but firmly: "I know, I could tell, I could sense. You've had a double mastectomy and it only makes you more desirable to me."

And then we "do it" and laugh. And I go home. All right, so that's not the worst.

But I want to go in that bar. I want to have a drink, and sit there and see what happens. All I can be is embarrassed or ignored. What do I have to lose?

I put the plastic cover over my old portable typewriter, and said to no one: "I am going. I am just fucking going!" I put on my big red down coat that made my head look so small and went.

Fanelli's is one of the last holdouts in otherwise overchic, overatmosphered, over-laid-back, pushed-forward SoHo. It has an old neon sign, an authentic long ornate bar, terrible wooden chairs and tables, the smell of brown liquor, an original dirty-white, small-tiled floor like your old bathroom . . . remember? And God bless the food. Thick tomato sauces, greasy sausages, overcooked vegetables, and iceberg lettuce . . . remember them? A few white-wine drinkers find their way there sometimes, but mostly it's real painters, dancers, shopowners, actors, and good neighborhood drunks who are there. I had even seen some telephone repairmen, UPS deliverymen, and construction types, so I figured if I didn't find Alan Bates, then at least I'd hook up with Charles Bronson . . . on one of his good days.

It was about three o'clock in the afternoon, and it wasn't too crowded. I could not get up the courage to stand at the bar, so I took a table, right next to the bar. I had forgotten to bring the lone-woman's appendage—a magazine or book—so I was stuck staring. I ordered a Jack Daniel's on the rocks and meatballs on a hero roll. It was very important, I felt, to present the right image—lusty, involved, troubled. Not a pampered housewife, resting after shopping or gallery going. I sipped at my drink and pushed around the meatballs while I tried to locate the object of my fantasy, or anyone else's for that matter. I remembered once hearing about a well-known photographer who was notorious for all the women he slept with wherever he was and whenever he wanted. His secret was simple. He asked almost everyone all the time, and even if he got eight turndowns that meant two yesses. So I said to myself, Which one is my first turndown? Yoo-hoo, Mr. No Sale, reveal yourself by some sign. Come on, guys, give me a sign.

At the bar, a crusty old gray beero scratched his rusty zipper. O.K., next. The bartender inclined his large flushed head toward me: "Another one, lady?" Two gay guys at the next table borrowed my ashtray. So far so good.

I finished my drink, sucked on the ice, took out my mirror, checked the color of the scar between my eyebrows, went to the ladies' room and didn't pee. When I came out, I ordered another drink and looked at the new guy in town. He was a young, thin, long-nosed kid with great dark blue eyes . . . and I realized that he was probably the same age as my son.

FOURTEEN

I can't tell you how many fittings it took to get the dress just right. It was clear, bright red, shiny silk, with a small and tasteful self-pattern. It had a high neck—so what else is new?—padded shoulders, a dropped waist, and then three tiers of ruffles. It was very short, and moved to beat the band when I moved. A perfect zazzy performing dress. Cynthia designed it, and we both were so frustrated during the endless fittings that we wanted to shriek. I didn't let on. She didn't let on. And the wonderful woman who was making it didn't let on. I made a few of my, by now, stale body jokes, but the truth was, none of us was sure that I could be dressed to look theatrical, sexy, comfortable, relaxed, and . . . normal . . . tilt . . . normal!

Nothing must show, the prosthesis mustn't move around. The lights would be powerful. People would be sitting very close and on three sides of the stage. I work physical, you know what I mean? I'm not a subdued songstress. I'm not a chilly chanteuse. I don't read quaint verse. I carry on. I sing and dance . . . vitality a specialty . . . was a specialty . . . We'll just see now, won't we?

So, we would get together, Cynthia, the seamstress, and I,

every two or three days, because I was scheduled to open in barely a week. The dress was made and remade. Standing in front of the mirror there, at Cynthia's house, being pinned and unpinned, staring at myself, gave me the sweats, the bends, the pip. Meanwhile, every day I would rehearse in our SoHo studio with Eric, the wonderful pianist, arranger, singer, I had worked with so often before. He didn't know anything about my illness. I couldn't tell him. Why? . . . Because his mother had died from the same thing the first year I met him, and he was still reeling. He was young, sensitive.

We got on wonderfully. We worked together with mutual appreciation, with humor, but I knew that I was in the maternal mold for him. I just couldn't have watched him having to deal with two women and two blah blahs and you know exactly what I mean! So I'd have to go into the bathroom, when my arms really got tired, so I could do some stretching. And I pretended to have a virus so I could sit down fairly often, because he was used to my rehearsing three or four hours at a clip, with my feet never touching the ground.

My voice was coming back with strength and I was still funny . . . sometimes. I so love to rehearse that when I go to heaven— which may be in about thirty-seven minutes—I'm going to do nothing but rehearse. I'll find Glenn Miller, round up the Count, the Duke, the Fats, and sing my chops off (whatever that means).

There was another problem. I was going to open and close with a song by Gretchen Cryer and Nancy Ford that I had sung in the show *I'm Getting My Act Together and Taking It on the Road.* It had certain lyrics that—every time I came to them—really turned on ye old tear ducts. Eric thought I was a method singer. I couldn't control the tears.

The lyrics were: "And I don't know what's coming. But this new day feels fine. 'Cause I woke up this morning and the face in the mirror was mine . . . Happy Birthday!" The song was about self-discovery and renewal. The "Act" was really shaping up. It seemed easier to put together songs and material, because I had my own subtext going. I was writing two shows in one. For the paying customers, it would be a blend of up tunes, down tunes, imitations, self-deprecating wit. (It's my party and I'll boast if I want to.) But to my friends, doctors, and country persons, it would be a saga, S.A.G.A. . . . and a miracle if I could bring it off so soon . . . so late . . . so what.

All right, *this is how it went:* There was a big audience out there in the club waiting for me . . . for me . . . for me . . . The saintly woman who "did" my hair at my wedding was doing the same style more or less, so many years later. It was hard for her to move, the dressing room was tiny, hot, and dirty and next to the customers' bathroom. So you had to be quiet, and also make sure not to pee too late or you'd run into your fans. The room was so small, and there were so many flowers, that I didn't open the wrappings. It looked like a floral delivery truck instead of a festive dressing room. I was profoundly terrified. I drank quarts and quarts of water (no ice, please), cups and cups of tea (a little lemon and honey, please), and sips and sips of bourbon—all at

Showbill® is a registered trademark of Playbill Incorporated, New York City. Used by permission.

the same time. Well, that does make one have to pee. So someone had to stand guard and make sure no one was going in or
out of the "rest room" (whoever rests there anyway?) while I
dashed in and out, in hot rollers, and a hot kimono.

The stage manager called the well-known "fifteen minutes."
No way. This is a terrible mistake. Who needs this? What am I
proving? What's this *I'll Cry Tomorrow* shit? Who do you have to
fuck to get off this planet? What if I raise my arm in a gesture
and I wince? What if it doesn't raise? What if my falsie falls?
Doesn't my hair look thin? My throat is closed up. How the hell
am I supposed to breathe? It feels so tight. Who will help me
into my dress? I can't let them see. I don't remember the opening lyrics. Where is it written that you have to be brave? I want a
doctor. Is there a doctor in the house? There is. There are. Oh,
oh, I want my mother . . . my mommy . . . my husband . . . my
bed . . . I want my old-time opening-night nerves. Who needs
these elaborate, macabre embellishments? I'll put some more
blush on. I look so fucking pale. Who cares? I care. I care so
much. I don't want to be good, for someone who has cancer, I
want to be really good. Don't you see? Don't you understand?
Make it go away. Make it last year. . . . *Here I go.*

The music was playing—my darling Eric and the cutest acous-
tical bass player in the West. The stage manager announced my
name over the PA. The spotlight hit me. Yes . . . yes . . . that's
really the way it happens. The maître d' walked me through the
tables. I couldn't see too well. There were a lot of "Yeahs!" A lot
of applause. My smile was frozen. My eyes were filling. I could
tell Cynthia's "yeah." I could make out Bobbie's posture . . . husband, kids, Betty B., Gloria . . . Oh my God . . . Dr. Surgeon,
Dr. Oncologist . . . with wives, with friends. Lots of other
people. Lots of pros, lots of press, smiling, bowing. O.K.,
sugar plum, this is it. Time to open the old mouth and connect,
connect.

The song started coming out, a little too nervous, but O.K.
"Concentrate on the music." It got better. I got through "those"
lyrics without sentimentality. Good applause, but they weren't
comfortable yet. I had to put friends and strangers at ease. That
was the name of the performing game. The second number was

a quiet, delicate but sexy ballad. I hadn't felt sexy in a year, but goddamnit, I did now. I felt pretty, oh so pretty. The red dress felt great. I could tell it looked great. My hips and legs behaved as if they hadn't been sick a day in their lives.

From then on it was the real tumble forward. Seamless. Real laughs. Real attention. Real rapport. It was my fake-ending song. Big response. Someone started the ever-popular standing ovation. Jesus Christ . . . It was cool Dr. Surgeon. Someone ringside was looking at me like a rapt kid at a ball game—honest to God, it was even cooler Dr. Oncologist. I had to do my last song, the first song, cyclical, you know. This time I didn't give a damn. I let it all happen. I threw my arms up. I've won God damn it don't you see? Can't you tell? . . . "And I don't know what's coming but this new day feels fine, 'cause I woke up this morning . . . and the face in the mirror was mine . . . Happy Birthday!"

EPILOGUE

BETTER
Lyrics by Ed Kleban

I've been fat.
I've been thin.
Thin is better.

I've been out.
I've been in.
In is better.

March 19, 1988, my birthday

I would never have sat down, or even stood up, to write a "memoir," an "autobiography," or "personal history" of my life had it not been shocked and rearranged.

I wrote at first because I had to, then because I wanted to, and now I think it's right to tell you the good things that have happened since, and are still happening.

Adolph is still Hungarian and devoted. He and his partner, Betty, are working on a new musical for Broadway. My son is writing a screenplay. My daughter just came back from Toledo, Ohio, where she made her professional debut as Angel in the musical *Best Little Whorehouse in Texas*.

Ron Barron, an ex-teacher who is now an unusual and caring manager, saw my performance that special evening at the nightclub. He didn't know anything about my medical history and when I told him, it made him even more determined to help me with my career. He started by looking for roles on, off, and even under Broadway. He discovered that people were sympathetic and would hire me for short gigs but the buzz was that I couldn't possibly do long rehearsals and eight performances a week.

André Bishop of Playwrights Horizons and playwright Wendy Wasserstein took a chance on me. I went into a workshop production of the musical *Miami,* written by Wendy with a score by Jack Feldman and Bruce Sussman. I played a somewhat stereotypical Jewish mother.

The show opened during one of the coldest winters New York ever had. The crowded dressing rooms were in the basement of the theater and it was a long, freezing climb up and down three sets of steep stairs to change clothes between scenes. It was about two months after Adam's wedding and my ankle was still mending from the fracture. Many nights it would swell—from the stair steps or the minimal dancing my part required. We rehearsed new pages or staging every day for the entire six-week run while doing the eight shows, because it was a workshop production. I pushed myself, and tried to improve my performance until the last show.

Fran Kumin, who was casting for Neil Simon's new play, *Broadway Bound,* was at one of the performances. She asked me to read the part of Aunt Blanche for Neil and director Gene Saks. It seemed to go well, but as in all the days of old, they asked me to read yet again, this time in an outfit and fur coat in "forties matron" style. Inwardly I groaned my never-perfected groan; outwardly I chirped my never-perfected, "Sure, love to . . . great!" Twenty-five years ago at the *Subways* audition, I had been asked to come back wrapped in a towel. Now Neil and Gene wanted to see me completely covered. The Lord she work in unmysterious ways.

When I went back, I did the best reading I was capable of and then I waited for about another month to find out I had been cast.

Gene Saks and I broke down Blanche's seven-minute scene in rehearsals, as if it were a three-act play. Unlike many shows I've been connected with, this play remained virtually unchanged. The process from rehearsal to out-of-town openings to the Broadway opening was seamless, and the play was a deserved great success. I felt that I got better and better and continued growing into the character long after the opening had passed.

At every performance, I dressed early in my extremely heavy, authentic forties, genuine mink coat, fur-trimmed rubber booties, and bulky red wool suit. With my sensible brown hat anchored to my lacquered pompadour, I would stand behind one of the flats on the stage a long time before my entrance and listen to my "family" and the play so that I could feel a part of the world they were creating. The preparation was the longest and most detailed I had ever done for a part; it lasted longer than the scene. The audience had to get to know Blanche's history quickly.

Seven or eight minutes later I was finished and I had a two-hour wait until the curtain call, which I had to take in full costume and makeup. The waiting time was the real test of my creativity—filling the hours without going nuts. I had a fairly large dressing room and I loaded it with electronic stuff from every discount house from Crazy Eddie to Mildly Disturbed 47th Street Photo. The thrill of all that was fleeting . . . eighty TV channels that I couldn't focus on . . . a whizzy little typewriter that I couldn't finish my book on . . . classical tapes that I couldn't concentrate on. The problem was, of course, that in my tiny actress's heart, I knew there was a play going on and I wasn't there. By twenty of nine when my scene was over, the very shank of the evening, I was raring to go, full the of well-known adrenaline, and nothing to do with it. So I started wandering the streets of the West Forties theater district. I felt like one of the street people. After a while, the panhandlers and pushers who shared my territory would give me a cheery "Yo" and "Hi, honey" nightly.

Sometimes I'd go to Sardi's, directly across from the theater on Forty-fourth, where Adolph had taken me on our first date;

Charlie's, an actors' hangout on Forty-fifth; or Orso, a terrific restaurant on Forty-sixth Street, where I'd have a little dinner alone, with Adolph, or whoever I could rope in for this odd stolen hour and a half. I stayed with the show for about a year and left with the rest of the wonderful actors who made up the original cast.

I've been poor.
I've been rich.
Rich is better.

Fancy,
Or not a stitch—
Which is better?

Toward the end of my run in *Broadway Bound*, I was asked by Paul Rauch, the producer of the popular daytime drama "One Life to Live," to do five guest appearances on the show, playing Renée Divine, an ex-madam from Nevada. I had never done a soap before, and flamboyant Renée was such a far cry from Aunt Blanche that it was irresistible. I have always wondered, as do most of you, probably, how the cast members learn their lines on the soaps every day. The week I started there were no TelePrompTers or any "memory helpers," so it was cold ham I was forced to serve up.

I had a good time with Renée right from the beginning. She was a shrewd, smart ex-hooker with a heart of steel, and here's the good part. . . . She was an attractive, sexy woman of my age. In her guise, I had my first middle-years kissing scene with the devilishly attractive Asa Buchanan (played by the devilishly attractive Phil Carey), and guess what shifty Hungarian just happened to wander onto the set as we were taping that moment? Anyway, Renée seemed to catch on and I became a semiregular, appearing once or twice a week for about six months. Renée talked like Martha Vail from *Subways* and she dressed like my very own mother did (and how she thought I should).

So I put on large earrings and the leopard and tiger print

fabrics that my mother loved wearing all the time and I could almost hear her saying, "Now you look like a million dollars, like a movie star." One night a long time ago I was describing her and her clothes on the Johnny Carson show and I mentioned that I called her Tiger Lily. Even as recently as yesterday somebody remembered that . . . and her.

> I've been healthy and in pain.
> Pain is reason to complain.
> Ask someone who's been insane.
> Sane is better.

"One Life to Live" gave me renewed television visibility and around Christmas of 1987 I was called to California to read for a new prime-time television series. I flew back and forth and read for Universal and CBS. Ron had to force me to keep making these trips. He even flew out with me to see that I didn't get cold feet. He knew that I wanted the part very badly but old neuroses neither die young nor fade away, they keep coming back like a song or like old clichés.

On a Friday, I got the part of Ginny Hale but there was one dicey moment. The next Monday, on the first day of rehearsal, a doctor appeared on the set to give the series regulars physical exams for insurance. I thought my health had ceased being an issue for me, but I realized that I was afraid they would turn me down, and that I would not only be out of this show that I so much wanted but would be "uninsurable" for any other long-running prime-time jobs. When the medical questionnaire was passed out before the exam, I was horrified to have to check the box marked "cancer." I was tempted to lie and see what happened but I didn't. For days, every time I saw the producers talking, I thought, They're trying to figure out how to fire me. Oh, how I wish I could tell you that I have now become relaxed, cheerful, centered, mature, smart, demonless, and thin. . . .

The show, by the way, is called "Coming of Age."